BEAUTY
FROM ASHES

BEAUTY FROM ASHES

DONNA SPARKS

BL BRIDGE
LOGOS

Newberry, FL 32669

Bridge-Logos
Newberry, FL 32669

Beauty from Ashes:
My Story of Grace
by Donna Sparks

Printed in the United States of America.

Library of Congress Catalog Card Number: 2017912209

International Standard Book Number: 978-1-61036-252-8

Cover/Interior design by Kent Jensen | knail.com

All Scripture quotations, unless otherwise indicated, are taken from the Holy Bible, New International Version®, NIV®. Copyright ©1973, 1978, 1984, 2011 by Biblica, Inc. Used by permission of Zondervan. All rights reserved worldwide. www.zondervan.com The "NIV" and "New International Version" are trademarks registered in the United States Patent and Trademark Office by Biblica, Inc.

Scripture quotation marked (NLT) are from the *Holy Bible, New Living Translation* ®, copyright © 1996, 2004 by Tyndale Charitable Trust. Used by permission of Tyndale House Publishers. All rights reserved

Scripture quotations marked (KJV) are from the King James Version of the Bible.

Literary Agent and Editor:
L. Edward Hazelbaker
11907 S. Sangre Road
Perkins, OK 74059
E-mail: l.edward@thewornkeyboard.com

VP 11-01-17

ENDORSEMENT BY DR. WAYNE NORTON

PEOPLE PRAY FOR God to give them leaders who will not camouflage the truth but, instead, dare to be honest and open with them. Donna Sparks is proving herself to be a leader who is up to that task. In *Beauty from Ashes: My Story of Grace*, Donna reveals her honest journey of faith, and that journey provides a message of God's hope for us all. When God calls an individual to do something for Him, He will confirm that calling. And Donna's *story of grace* shows that her call to ministry has been assured by God the Father, appropriated by God the Son, and anointed by God the Holy Spirit.

Every chapter of this book will open readers to a new dimension and directive of God's grace. Those who dare to read this book with open hearts, open minds, and open spirits will find blessings of grace awaiting them. In revealing the process of her own spiritual and ministerial growth, Donna boldly declares her personal testimony and hides none of her weaknesses or struggles. That spirit of honesty introduces us to what the grace of God can accomplish in our own lives and ministries. Every chapter testifies that the Holy Spirit can and will transform lives for God's glory.

Donna Sparks writes with a "holy boldness" that comes only to a person who is absolutely absorbed with and controlled by the Holy Spirit. God is glorified as Donna teaches and proclaims one Bible truth after another and applies them to the times in which we live. I encourage you to read this book. Then let this book read you, and let God's Word speak as the Holy Spirit opens to you a powerful message, miracle, and manifestation of His grace.

Grace awaits you in a personal experience with our triumphant and Triune God. Grace reminds all believers and church leaders that God chooses whom He uses. And, truly, God has chosen Donna Sparks and used her to write this "must read" book to encourage us to see that the life of every born-again believer is a *story of grace.*

—Dr. Wayne Norton
Founder/Executive Director
Hope for Your Day Ministries
Claremore, Oklahoma

DEDICATION

TO MY LORD and Savior Jesus Christ, who has . . .

    Loved me,

    Redeemed me,

    Carried me,

    Comforted me,

    Guided me, and,

    Forgiven me—countless times.

And to my husband Bryan, who, like Christ, has . . .

    Respected me,

    Believed in me,

    Supported me,

    Encouraged me,

    Provided for me, and,

    Demonstrated leadership—with humility.

—DS

FOREWORD

WHEN DONNA SPARKS showed up for our television interview I was amazed by her humble and gracious spirit. Her family had driven for many hours to get there, and she was surely tired, yet before me stood a most lovely and exuberant presence. She lit up the room. There was a certain delicate strength about her, and I immediately loved this woman.

As cameras rolled and she began to share her incredible journey, I could see how the testing of her faith through fiery trials had brought about gold in her soul. It was clear that the Holy Spirit had used her suffering, by many means, to do a powerful work in her spirit. Donna had become a force against the darkness. Little did I know the price she had paid to get there.

As I read the incredible, sometimes supernatural stories in this book, I was reminded of how intricate and calculated God's plan is for each of us. He uses the pain, the rejections, the betrayals, the losses, and the failures to weave His grace through our journeys. As Donna strategically maps out the story of how grace rescued her again and again, the reader cannot help but be encouraged that if God would so miraculously intervene for her, then He will also do it for us.

Who among us does not face the common assault of the enemy telling us that we just can't do it? In this book you will find wisdom on how to navigate the inevitable pitfalls and difficulties we will encounter as God moves us into higher and more spacious places of influence. Leadership is not for the faint of heart. Donna exemplifies courage when she didn't think she had it in her to do so. She shows us with such vulnerable authenticity how feelings of unworthiness and fears of being incapable of fulfilling God's strategic plans are common to us all.

My spirit resonated with some of the challenges Donna faced as God expanded her territory. What do we do when others are jealous of our calling? How do we handle losing valued friendships because people cannot handle our promotions from the Lord? Donna teaches us to hear the still, small voice of God and to walk in obedience to its nudging while navigating the sometimes treacherous waters of advancement.

There are not many who can use the art of story to unearth truth as profoundly as this book's author has done. It was like discovering treasure as I opened every chapter and considered the wisdom recorded on each page. And as I read I paused to consider the similarities of God's patterns and principles for victory.

We all face accusations. We all come up against barriers that threaten to derail us. We know the sting of someone not believing in us or the uneasiness of not believing in ourselves. How do we steady our grip and anchor our destinies in these storms? Donna has shared her own calling and training for ministry with such honest clarity that it translates answers to our questions right into the box of tools we need to help us steer through such challenges.

The calling God has placed upon Donna is profound. And I'm so glad she was willing to allow her life to become this *open book* about both the joyous and challenging parts of her successful stride. It is like a spring of water to those who thirst for knowledge, and every page in it is a gem and worthy of your investment of time to read.

Your own story of grace will be enhanced by the richness of sharing Donna's insights into God's priceless love and commitment to His children. *Beauty from Ashes: My Story of Grace* is simply a magnificent weaving of the Lord's awe-inspiring kindness.

—Laura-Lynn Tyler Thompson
Co-host of 700 Club Canada

TABLE OF CONTENTS

INTRODUCTION

MANY TIMES WHEN I've been invited to speak, people in attendance have asked me or my ministry partners if I have a book containing my "story of grace." Since the relating of my personal testimony touches on so many different issues, it's common for attendees to tell me they know someone who they wish could have been with them to hear me tell about my experiences. They say their acquaintances, friends, or family members could really relate to my testimony and benefit from a book containing my story.

Although I find no joy in writing about the failures that are part of my life's story—for I clearly hate and regret them—I eventually came to feel that more people might, indeed, benefit from reading the lessons I learned through them. So I undertook the task of recording what now makes up the contents of the book you are holding. I will be glad to hear one day that this book not only helped others avoid making the same mistakes that I made but also encouraged them in their Christian walk.

We all have occasional struggles, and, unfortunately, we all make mistakes. We've all been in situations and through seasons in life when we might not completely understand things, and sometimes those things can be so challenging that we may feel like we won't even survive them. But because we are in Christ, we do survive. And people who become and remain faithful to Jesus not only survive but come to thrive as our wonderful Lord uses the circumstances in our lives to bring us victory and hope.

In the midst of our problems, Satan, the enemy of our souls, loves to try to convince people who have failed that they have no hope. But he is a thief and a liar; we who have failed most certainly do have hope, and we have a sure future through Jesus Christ. As the leader of a women's jail ministry program, I have had the privilege of ministering to many women who in themselves find hope hard to maintain. They feel trapped by their failures and disappointments. And our souls' enemy wants to keep them there.

I have great compassion for all who have made mistakes and feel bound by their past lives. In part, that compassion clearly comes from my own experiences with failures and frailties. But that feeling of compassion is hotly driven by the Holy Spirit; for He has shown me where the hope they need is found.

Hope is birthed in us through the love and compassion of Jesus Christ. I have experienced it. I have experienced the greatest love ever known—the love of Jesus! And I am driven to see others know the breadth of that love and live in the hope it brings.

God has worked amazing miracles and provided many blessings in my life, and I know He wants to do the same for others. I want others to discover the same wonderful confidence I have come to know as a result of what God has done for me. I want others to come to know Jesus as savior and friend. I want others to find what they need in Him. And with this book I desire to reach out to readers of all backgrounds to inspire, encourage, and build them up in the Faith.

I pray that you—no matter where you may be in your walk—will find something you can relate to in this book, and I pray that the Holy Spirit will use it to encourage and instruct you. I pray it will inspire your faith and cause you to realize you are never alone in this Christian journey we call Discipleship.

If you fail in your attempts to live and minister for Jesus (and I'm not just appealing to those who feel called to pulpit ministry), you definitely are not alone. It will encourage you to remember that others failed, too, and lived to tell about it. And it will absolutely bless you and inspire your faith to know how the trusting believers who failed so miserably in the past did not allow those failures to stop them in their pursuit of God. They looked up; they cried out to the Lord; they repented; and they were heard.

God hears the cries of the disappointed and crushed. He has compassion for them and responds to those who acknowledge their failures and cry out to Him for restoration and help. If we are to be people of faith, if we are going to please the Lord, we must keep getting up and keep going when we fail God or generally make a mess here and there in our life's journey. We can't stay down!

As you read this book I want you to know that I have already prayed for you. Regardless of how you may feel, God's *not* finished with you. If you have experienced failure, you *can* survive it. God really *does* have great plans for you![1]

You *can* find forgiveness and restoration through the love of Jesus and through God's wonderful gift to us of the Holy Spirit. You *can* arise and do anything God calls you to do. Now get to it!

—Donna

---

1   "For I know the plans I have for you," declares the Lord, "plans to prosper you and not to harm you, plans to give you hope and a future" (Jeremiah 29:11).

CHAPTER 1

LIFE WITHOUT CHRIST

There is no darker place on earth than what exists in the depths of a heart without Christ. —DS

ALMOST EVERY TIME I am invited to speak I start my message by providing to my audience a little information on my background. I certainly don't do that because I'm proud of my past (for truthfully, there is nothing I'm more ashamed of), but I do it because I am committed to being transparent with people as I minister to them.

Sometimes people need to see living, breathing proof that there is hope for their lives to be resurrected from *the ashes*. Perhaps you feel like your life has become a lifeless ash heap. As you begin reading this book I want you to know that I believe God can bring you out of the ashes to live again, because God did that for me. And if revealing my past experiences can be used by the Holy Spirit to encourage others, then I gladly share my testimony.

I was born and raised in church. I had Christian parents who made sure that my brother and I were in church every time the doors were open. I was saved when I was nine years old, and I really was a decent young person throughout my early life and teen years. I tried to follow Christ daily all during those years.

As most young Christian girls do, I had my own personal dreams of finding a *Prince Charming* in the form of a Christian husband. I dreamed of having a big beautiful wedding and a nice house with a white picket fence. You get the picture.

So when by the age of twenty-three I found myself divorced—not just once but twice—you can imagine what I thought of my dreams and, especially, my own life. I was not just disappointed in myself, though, I was disappointed in God. I felt like God had let me down, and before long I stopped caring about what He had to say to me.

When Christians stop listening to the still, small voice of the Holy Spirit,[2] their relationships with Jesus can deteriorate very quickly. And when people stop responding to God's wise

---

2 "And he said, Go forth, and stand upon the mount before the Lord. And, behold, the Lord passed by, and a great and strong wind rent the mountains, and brake in pieces the rocks before the Lord; but the Lord was not in the wind: and after the wind an earthquake; but the Lord was not in the earthquake: And after the earthquake a fire; but the Lord was not in the fire: and after the fire a still small voice.

"And it was so, when Elijah heard it, that he wrapped his face in his mantle, and went out, and stood in the entering in of the cave" (1 Kings 19:11-13a KJV).

In the New International Version "still small voice" is interpreted as "a gentle whisper."

instructions and voice of reason, they soon find themselves yielding to deceptive influences. I learned that first-hand.

The enemy of our souls is quick to take advantage of every opportunity to fill the voids in our lives that exist where God is not welcome. The Lord may speak to us in a still, small voice, but that's not how the devil speaks. He seemingly steps in with a megaphone as he attempts to drown out God's voice, and he starts doing everything within his power to lure us away from the One who loves us—the one who wants the very best for us.

Satan's intent is to steal us away from our savior, kill the relationships we have with Christ, and totally destroy us.

The thief comes only to steal and kill and destroy; I have come that they may have life, and have it to the full. (John 10:10)

I had to change jobs after my second divorce, and I soon found myself working extremely long hours. Before long I was skipping church. My prayer life was practically non-existent, and I rarely picked up my Bible. Temptation began to sweep in from every angle. My friends began to ask me to go out and party with them. At first that wasn't something I would even consider. But after I drifted away from church, I soon began listening to the enemy's lies—as I believe he began to say things to me like, "What has God done for you? You would be better off doing things your own way. God hasn't done a very good job with your life so far."

I found myself growing increasingly angry at God. More and more I became an angry young woman. I started wondering why God had allowed things to go so horribly wrong in my life. You see, Satan had used his influence to convince me it was all God's fault, and I was just an innocent bystander. After all, if God really loved me everything would be bright, happy, and carefree all the days of my life, right?

Wrong!

Satan likes for us to think it's all about us—that the world should revolve around us. In fact, that is one of the best delusions he promotes in our society today. Go to *Burger King* and "Have it your way". *L'Oréal* says you should use their products because "You're worth it." *McDonalds* says, "You deserve a break today." If Satan can convince us to focus on ourselves all the time, it is easy to influence us to become self-absorbed, self-serving people who only care about what's happening in our own little worlds.

God wants us to have compassion for others and not be consumed with our own motives, desires, and plans. Seeing that we are sinners saved only by grace, remembering that we truly don't *deserve* anything but death and hell will help us to keep from falling into the trap of selfishness. And in all His mercy and unfathomable love, God developed a plan for us to be saved not only from a life of selfishness but also from that destiny to which it leads.

God became flesh. The only begotten Son of God took our place in paying the awful debt that our sins built up. Jesus died for our sins and bore our shame. Christ paid an awful price to redeem us and give us a life truly worth living. And we have the nerve to think we deserve more?

But influencing me to become self-absorbed is exactly how the enemy got to me. It was easier for me to turn my back and walk away from God after I decided that He was to blame for all my problems. And that is what I did. I started partying and drinking. I partied and drank more and more.

After some time I noticed there was something about me that seemed different from the friends I partied with. At some point they would stop drinking, but I couldn't. I didn't stop until I had either passed out or was hanging over a toilet in some nasty, public restroom.

And it got worse, much worse. Before long I was stopping by the package store and buying alcohol on a daily basis. I began drinking at home alone, every day. There were days I went to work drunk, and I had no idea how I even got there. Many times I would come home on the weekends and have no idea what time I got home, where my car was parked, or even if I had driven it home. I was living a miserable life, but at that point all I cared about was alcohol. It was my new best friend.

One day a new guy was hired where I worked. I wasn't really interested in dating anyone—basically because I didn't want to give up my alcohol. But luckily (as I felt at the time), Bryan wasn't a Christian. He didn't care if I drank. Morally, though, he was a better person than I was; he just didn't know God. He didn't party, drink, or do drugs; but he didn't care if I did, so we got along fine.

We dated two months and then got married. The first year was a nightmare. We fought almost constantly, and it was mostly my fault. I stayed drunk all the time, and the alcohol caused many arguments that would never have taken place otherwise. But I didn't care. I didn't care about anything or anyone but myself, and things were about to get a whole lot worse.

The more I drank, the more I got depressed. And as depression began to increase, so did my consumption of alcohol. I was in a downward spiral from which I couldn't escape. As time went on, Bryan and I began to discuss having children. We had been married three years at that time, and I wouldn't say we were trying to conceive, but we were not exactly trying to avoid it either. I decided to see my doctor, who told me that I most likely would not be able to have children. After that, I was even more depressed. I had always wanted children.

I had a panic attack one afternoon at work. I had never experienced one before, and I literally thought I was going to die. It scared me, but it scared Bryan even more. He immediately took me to my family doctor, and the doctor prescribed antidepressants and *Xanax*. This was wonderful news for me! Having an addictive personality, I ended up consuming the *Xanax* pills like they were jelly beans. And guess what? I became even more depressed.

Bryan was doing everything he could to make me happy. He bought me everything he thought my heart could desire, including a brand new red Mustang GT. It was a beautiful car, and it was loaded with everything a Mustang could have. I was happy for a day or two, but alcohol and depression soon brought me back down. I was absolutely miserable.

One morning I got up and went shopping for shoes. I had taken at least half the bottle of *Xanax* pills with a big drink of alcohol, and I was on my way. I went into the shoe store and found four pairs of shoes I really liked. I couldn't decide which ones I liked the most, though, so I eventually bought all four and left the store. When I got back in my Mustang, I picked up the bottle of *Xanax*, swallowed the remaining pills with another big drink of alcohol, and drove off.

Instead of driving back home, I turned and headed out on the interstate. I have no idea why I even did such a thing. As I was driving, it was as if Satan jumped up on my shoulder and began telling me how pathetic I was.

These thoughts began to run through my head: "Bryan will eventually leave you for someone else; you are totally worthless, so he would be better off without you. You have totally made a mess out of your life. God is so disgusted with you. You are a loser; everyone else would be better off without you if you were gone!"

I glanced down at my speedometer and noticed I was going 130 mph. The car felt like it was barely touching the road. It felt so light—almost as if it were floating. It was in those next few moments that an overwhelming thought entered my mind that I should just end it all.

It was as if Satan whispered in my ear, "One quick jerk of the wheel, and this could all be over."

I had never in my life considered suicide as an option—ever! I always thought nothing could be bad enough to make me even consider such a thing. But in that moment I decided to end it. I didn't see any other cars on the road, and I decided to aim my car at the next concrete overpass. I soon had the overpass in sight, and I pressed the accelerator to the floor.

I wish I could tell you what happened next, but I can't remember. I woke up in my bed at home, and I wasn't sure how I got there. When I pulled back the covers, I saw that I was fully dressed in what I had worn earlier that day. I started asking myself if it could have possibly been a dream. But, it seemed so real!

I knew what to do. I decided to go out to my car and see if the shoes were there. I opened the door of my Mustang, and there in the back seat were the four pairs of shoes. And in the front seat lay the empty *Xanax* bottle and empty liquor bottle.

It most definitely did happen!

"So, how did I get home?" I thought. I may never know the answer to that question, but I can say confidently now that however it happened it was simply by the grace of God that I lived and now write to tell you about it.

Bryan and I were at work a week or so later, and we had a huge argument. This wasn't unusual, but that particular argument was more intense than any I could remember. I was screaming at him, and I felt so much rage! I couldn't figure out what was wrong or why I was so furious. Bryan had to stay late for a meeting, so I went home. Later I called and asked him to pick up a pregnancy test on the way home. He asked why on earth I would want one, and I told him I just felt weird.

We had dinner and watched TV, and honestly, I had completely forgotten about the pregnancy test. Just before bed, though, Bryan asked why I wanted the test. I then went into the bathroom to take the test, and I could not believe my eyes. It was positive! I thought it had to be a faulty test, and since it was a two pack, I took the other one. Same answer—positive! I ran into the room and told Bryan he was going to be a daddy. We danced around laughing and happy, and then we began making phone calls to our parents.

The actual reality of it began to sink in after we went to bed. "I am going to be a mother! I am going to be responsible for the life of another human being!

I already loved the baby more than I could even believe, and I wanted the best for my child. I began to think about my own mother. She had raised me right. She taught me how to live a godly life and made sure I went to church. And then I began to think about what a lousy mother I was going to be.

But since my mother had, indeed, raised me in church, and because of all the things she did, in fact, teach me, I knew it didn't have to be that way. After all that pain and depression, and an actual attempt to end my life, I still knew where to go for help.

"What was I thinking?" I asked myself. I then decided I was going to go back to church. "But what is Bryan going to think about this?" I wondered.

The next morning, I said to Bryan, "I was thinking about going to church this Sunday. Would you want to go with me?"

He immediately said, "Sure!"

I was shocked. I never imagined it would be that easy.

The following Sunday we got up and got ready for church. I had picked a church where no one knew me. I wanted to go in and act like I was *OK*; and maybe somehow, perhaps by osmosis, I would leave clean. I knew that wasn't really how it worked, but I was still ashamed to admit how messed up I truly was.

When the pastor began to preach, it was as if he were reading my mail. Tears rolled down my face as he spoke, and I just thought, "Please, hurry up and give the altar call!"

When the pastor finally gave the invitation, I ran to that altar. I fell on my knees and said "God, I am so sorry. I have messed up so bad. Please forgive me and come back into my heart."

Peace flooded back into my heart in that very moment. The void within me that had been like a giant vacuum, sucking up all the terrible things the world had to offer, was now full of the love of Jesus.

I felt like I was home again. I looked over at Bryan, who was kneeling beside me, and he was crying his eyes out, too. It was one of the happiest moments of my life. I'm happy to say that upon leaving the church that day, my craving for alcohol was gone. I left the church with Jesus, and there is absolutely nothing that can satisfy the soul like Him.

Soon our darling, completely-healthy daughter was born, and of course she was the most beautiful baby in the world. And before she turned two, we found out that she was going to have a baby sister. Before we knew it, we had two perfect, beautiful daughters. We were a happy family; we were in church, and life was great.

After that, God moved us to Iowa, and I was not happy about it at all. I never wanted to go to Iowa; but before I knew it, we were buying a house there and looking for a Christian school for our first daughter. That move was far-detached from any of my plans; but I was there, and obviously God had a plan. I determined that I would just have to adjust.

Living in Iowa was very hard at first. We couldn't find a church that was anything close to what our church in Tennessee had been like. I was seriously homesick. Finally, though, God led us to a small Assembly of God church there in Iowa, and it soon became our new church home. I had no idea what was coming next, and if anyone had told me, I would never have believed the person anyway.

CHAPTER 2

REVENGE

I OFTEN HEAR people say that coffee smells much better than it tastes. Well I can assure you that revenge is like that. Revenge also sounds a lot more gratifying than it actually is. And participating in it can also lead to a lot more trouble than one could ever be prepared for!

When someone hurts us, or wrongs us, the response of our human nature may cause us to want to retaliate. That response puts us in a place of wanting to get even. With that attitude we think the sweet taste of revenge will be so refreshing. Yet when acted out, taking revenge for the wrongs done to us can leave us with an aftertaste of bitterness—and all too often a big mess to clean up.

My mom always told me, "Two wrongs don't make a right." But my response to her was often, "It may not make it right, but it will make me feel better!" We may feel like we are entitled to a bit of revenge after being hurt, but somehow taking revenge always seems to backfire for me. How about you?

Here's what the Bible says about revenge:

Do not take revenge, my dear friends, but leave room for God's wrath, for it is written: "It is mine to avenge; I will repay," says the Lord. (Romans 12:19)

God's Word tells us not to seek revenge, and there are several good reasons for that. But knowing what the Bible says about the issues of life doesn't always mean we will automatically follow the advice given to us in Scripture. I know that first hand. Believe me, I know what it's like to want revenge.

I go back a little farther in time now to relate to you the following account.

When my first husband brought his new girlfriend into the home we had shared, I was determined to get revenge. Of course my first inclination was to go there, drag her out of the house, and rearrange her teeth. I guess it was best for both of us that she didn't come to the door that day when I needed to go to the house. I was so full of rage! In my mind she had taken something that was mine. *She* had taken *my* husband; *she* had destroyed *my* marriage; *she* was the problem.

But as time went on, I began to realize it wasn't all her fault. As the old saying goes, "It takes two to tango." I eventually realized my ex-husband was the one I was really angry with. He was the one who had hurt me, and I was determined to hurt him back. Sweet revenge was soon to be mine!

Here's the background to how my plan developed:

I worked in a hair salon when my first husband Tom (not his real name) and I were dating. Many times Tom would come to the salon to have lunch with me. There was a tall, dark, handsome guy who frequented our little shop (I'll refer to him as Bill), and he always requested me to cut his hair. Of course being a business man, the most convenient time for Bill to get a haircut was during his lunch hour.

Bill was always cheerful and happy to chat with me during his appointments. I soon noticed that he was coming to get his hair cut much more frequently than before. And when he started coming once a week to get a haircut, I mentioned to him that there was barely any hair left to cut. It was obvious to me that he wasn't coming to the salon just to get a haircut anymore—even though I had made sure he knew I was unavailable.

It also became obvious to Tom that my haircuts were not Bill's only interest, and Tom began to be jealous of him.

Soon Bill purchased a tanning package so he could come in and use the tanning beds and talk to me before and after he tanned. That really made Tom angry. He absolutely despised Bill at that point. But soon Tom and I were married; Bill had moved to another state; and life was good.

That is, life was good until ten months later, when I found out about *her*.

Tom and I soon thereafter divorced; and after our divorce was final—after I had schemed for the longest time to figure out the best method of getting revenge over how I had been treated—it suddenly hit me. Tom hates Bill!

After a little investigation I was able to find out where Bill had relocated, and I even managed to get his new phone number. I called him. In my thoughts I was already envisioning the expression on Tom's face when he would hear that I was dating Bill.

This was going to be the best revenge ever.

Bill answered the phone when I called, and I asked him how he was doing. When I told him who I was, he said, "Oh, hi, how are you?"

I said, "I'm fine, even though I just went through a divorce."

I could hear the tone of his voice change as excitement filled the wave of his next few words. "I AM SO . . . *sorry*," he replied, trying not to sound too happy.

But it was too late for that. He asked me out right then, and we went on our very first date that same weekend.

"Take that Tom!" was what I thought.

Bill was a lot older than me, and I thought he was a man who was settled and had his head on straight. He continually showered me with elaborate gifts and constant compliments. He talked about how stupid Tom was for cheating on me; and he swore by the sun, moon, and stars, that if I were ever *his* wife, I would never need to worry about such a thing.

I was so disappointed in myself after the divorce, and I constantly asked myself; "What was wrong with *me* when Tom and I were together? Why wasn't I good enough for him? Was I too fat? Was I not smart enough, or funny enough? Why did he want someone else? Why not *me?*"

Bill was right there at that time to fill in every blank in my life of questions. I experienced a never-ending deluge of compliments from him, and his gushing mushiness made me feel so much better about myself. He did everything he could to make me feel special.

He sent me roses every week, and he bought elaborate gifts for me. Since he lived in another state, he drove over 100 miles every weekend just to take me out on dates. He took me to the finest restaurants, and he pretty-much promised me the world on a silver platter. I felt better, finally, and I began to regain some self-confidence. I felt secure with Bill.

So when he proposed seven months later it was no surprise to anyone that I said, "Yes!" Everyone thought he was perfect for me. I wasn't so sure he was perfect, but being with Bill was certainly better than being alone; and he *did* seem to really love me—and I loved him.

However, as soon as we left the wedding ceremony I knew I had made a horrible mistake. I had a strong sense of uneasiness. I thought I was making a good, sound decision about our marriage, but as I began to wake up beside a complete stranger in the following days I realized I had ignored some pretty crucial things.

It was literally only a matter of days before everything I knew about Bill began to change. Step by step I discovered every single thing he had told me had been a lie. All I thought I knew about him dissolved in the harsh reality of who he really was.

I found out that Bill had acquired a huge amount of debt while trying to put on an impressive front for me. And I discovered that he was full of lies. I think I could have dealt with *some* of the lies, but the most heart-wrenching lie that he told me was that he loved me. My life with him after we married felt nothing like love; and he certainly turned out not to be the man I had thought he was during the time we had been dating for seven months, and during our engagement for two more months.

Everything between us changed, and we both began doing battle on a daily basis with an arsenal of verbal weapons.

Every time the phone rang, I knew I was going to find out something even more devastating than the last bit of information I had learned about him. It felt like I was living in a nightmare, and I couldn't wake up. One night, after another terrible fight, Bill left. He was nowhere to be found for two weeks. He didn't come home; he didn't call; and I couldn't reach him on his cell phone. I finally talked to his employer, and he claimed Bill had taken a vacation.

After the two weeks were over, Bill showed up again and filed for divorce. While questioning why on earth this was happening to me again, I began to reflect on the only thing that caused me to look him up in the first place. You see, my sweet little plan of revenge had resulted in an absolute disaster. And my mistake of pursuing revenge brought to me the devastation of going through a second divorce before reaching the age of twenty-three.

If you go looking for trouble, you can rest assured that the enemy of our souls will make sure you find it! And while we can't blame the devil for all our troubles (we are, after all, responsible for our own decisions and our responses to temptation), he is an exploiter of human nature, and he will manipulate anything he can or anyone who will yield to his influence. Beware of yielding to his tricks!

I spent a lot of time trying to understand where I went wrong and how my second experience with marriage had been such a disaster. I am now convinced of the answer: I had not given myself time to heal. In all my pain and anger, I was focused only on seeking revenge. Things could have gone much differently if I had only left it all in God's hands to handle.

God knows how to deal with the toughest of situations. No relational problem that we might have is beyond His power to handle. We are too often irrational in the moments after we have been hurt or betrayed, but God is always rational. We can be prone to making bad decisions in our heartache, but God never makes bad decisions. We need to turn our troubles over to Him and rest in His ability to bring us justice.

It took a terrible experience for me to learn to trust God to represent me in times of challenge and trouble. Through it the Lord helped me learn a valuable lesson about the potential danger that exists in my own natural feelings of self-preservation and an all-too-human desire for retribution for the wrongs that I have—and still do sometimes—experience. Here is a verse from Scripture that I have learned to depend on. You can depend on it, too.

> *For the Lord your God is going with you! He will fight for you*
> *against your enemies, and He will give you victory!*
>   (Deuteronomy 20:4 NLT).

You see, God cares enough about us to be concerned about the things we go through in life, and it is an act of faith for us to trust Him to fight our battles for us. Our natural tendency may be to lash out to make sure others feel the same pain we feel. But that is not God's way. And we will only suffer more than we have already suffered if we make it ours.

We cannot always trust our own feelings and inclinations, but we can always trust God's. He not only knows how to save us, He knows how to help us deal with every circumstance in life. The way the Lord judges and brings justice may not be the way we would, but His way is the right way.

It will take both patience and faith for you to depend on the Lord to fight for you, but if you do, you will find out He does the best job. And you will find out that turning your pain over to Him and trusting Him was absolutely the best thing you could have done.

CHAPTER 3

THE ART OF SURRENDER

"I'm not good enough to do anything for God. If people only knew about my past, my failures, and what a mess I was..."

THIS IS EXACTLY what I said for many years.

When a visiting pastor came to speak at our church several years ago, he ended the service by having everyone come to the altar. He prayed for many people, but I'll never forget what he said when he prayed for me.

He said, "God has called you to be an evangelist."

I thought he was out of his mind. I shrugged off every word he said to me after that. My mind was too busy running through the events of my past. I thought, "If he only knew about my past, he would feel very silly for saying that God has called me to do these things!"

I knew that I was *all* right with God again. I had asked Him to forgive me for my sins, and I knew He had. I had turned away from my sins and was living my life for Him. The only problem was, I thought the Lord was probably still angry with me.

I had failed so miserably that I was sure He was at least really disappointed in me.

I'll never forget the Sunday morning when my pastor's wife walked up to me and my husband Bryan and told me about an upcoming women's conference. My mind began racing for excuses not to go! Spending the night in a hotel room with three other ladies I didn't know very well did not sound like my idea of a good time.

Before I could even think of a logical excuse, though, Bryan said, "Sure, how much is it?"

He already had his wallet out and was pulling out the money for registration. Immediately berating him in my mind, I thought, "I'm going to *KILL* you when we get out of here!" As soon as we were out of earshot, I asked him, "Why on earth would you do such a thing to me?"

He said, "You need to get out of the house and away from the kids for a weekend. It will do you some good."

I was furious.

Suitcase packed, makeup, purse, Bible—check! Out the door I went and off to the church to board the church van and speed away to the women's conference. *Oh joy!*

We arrived at the venue where the conference was being held and made our way up the aisle to our seats. Looking around, I didn't think I had ever seen that many women in one room. It was like the neighborhood coffee shop on free-coffee day! There must have been at least 500 ladies in that auditorium.

Soon after everyone found their seats, the worship team began to sing. The Presence of the Holy Spirit was so real in that place! We began to sing a simple song by William McDowell, called *I Give Myself Away*. Tears began to fill my eyes and slowly trickle down my cheeks as I listened to the words, "I give myself away, so You can use me."

With both arms lifted high, I prayed to my Father God in that tender private moment. I simply said, "God, I know I have failed you, and I know I have made some really bad mistakes. I'm sure I have disappointed you and made you cry, but if there is anything you can do with this broken life of mine, I give myself completely and entirely to you right now. If you have any use for me at all, I'm willing. I give myself away—to You!"

I can't describe the feeling I experienced at that moment. It was as if a whole barrel of warm love was poured down on me from Heaven all at once! I have never felt so loved in all my life. All I could do was weep, but I was weeping tears of joy. Real joy!

It was a wonderful service, and soon we were making our way back to the hotel to try to get rested for the next day. I think I was still basking in God's love when the sun came up the next morning. We four ladies took turns in the bathroom—hairdryers, curling irons, makeup bags, shoes, and perfume strewn throughout the room—and soon we were en route to the conference again.

That was a great day filled with awesome worship, interesting sessions, delicious food, and lots of laughter. But soon I was running out of steam, and my high heels were not being as friendly to me as they had been when I put them on that morning. We were beginning the last session, and the final speaker took the platform. She preached a good sermon, and she was just about to end the service when she turned to the host, and asked, "Is it ok if I pray for a couple of people?"

Well, of course it was; so she began to scan through the audience saying, "Where is she? I saw her earlier, and I knew God wanted me to pray for her."

I was thinking, "Good luck lady, this is a pretty large crowd!"

About that time her eyes fastened on the section I was sitting in (near the back), and she said, "You, sweetheart, come up here."

Obviously she was talking to someone else. "It couldn't be me," I thought as I looked around nervously.

"You there, with the sparkly stuff around your collar," she said, looking at me.

Now, I was really looking around me, and thinking, "There had better be someone else here with sparkly stuff on her blouse! Nope, just me; great!"

I can't tell you how I got out of that long narrow row of chairs and made it all the way down to the front of the auditorium. I'm sure I sounded like I was tap dancing all the way, because my legs were shaking so much.

As I cautiously made my way toward her, she began to pray for me. The very first thing she said was, "God said you didn't even want to come to this conference."

I thought skeptically, "Well, she got that right!" But as she continued, I knew God was using her to speak to me. There was no way she could have known what had been taking place in my mind that whole weekend. Those thoughts were between me and God alone.

She began to tell me that He had called me for His purposes, to do some awesome things. She then said, "You do not believe you are worthy to do anything for Him, but it is time for you to step out into the things of God."

At that point I was bawling like a baby. It was as if she had vanished into thin air, and I was only aware of my Heavenly Father speaking to me. I knew in that moment that He had called me, and He was confirming to me that He would use me.

I'm glad the Lord knows me so well. You see, I always had a lot of doubts. And I was always very skeptical about people who just suddenly received a word from God for someone. But that day, God showed me who He was—and still is. Not only is He our Father, but He also is our Friend! He cares about each one of us individually. He knows our thoughts, our fears, and our personalities. He knows everything about us—our mistakes, flaws, and failures. He has seen us at our best and at our very worst. God just knows us; and despite all of that, He loves us!

I worried for so long that I could never please God because I was so unworthy. I knew I could never be "good enough." But the Lord drew my mind to the Scriptures.

The Bible tells us that *"our righteous acts are as filthy rags"* (Isaiah 64:6). Through God's Word I finally came to realize that none of us are worthy. I finally understood. The wonderful part about the gospel message is that Jesus *is* worthy! *He* is righteous! And He loves us so much that He was willing to lay down His life and shed His blood to cover our filth.

He took all of our sins and filthiness upon himself. He carried that cross, was nailed to it, and died so we could be counted as blameless. As the precious blood of Jesus ran down and dripped on the ground around the Cross, atonement was made for all our sins—once and for all time.

When we repent and ask Him to be our savior and the Lord of our lives, His precious blood washes away all our ugly, black sin. We become as white as snow,[3] and we are covered by His righteousness! When God looks down at one of His redeemed ones, He no longer sees a person who is unworthy. He sees us through the righteousness of Christ Jesus, who alone *is* worthy.[4]

---

3   "'Come now, let us settle the matter,' says the Lord. 'Though your sins are like scarlet, they shall be as white as snow; though they are red as crimson, they shall be like wool'" (Isaiah 1:18).

4   "It is because of him that you are in Christ Jesus, who has become for us wisdom from God—that is, our righteousness, holiness and redemption"

When your sins have been forgiven and covered by the blood, the past need not define your future. Our lives today may still bear the effects of the decisions we made in the past, but God's focus for the redeemed is always on the futures that He has planned for them. If you know Jesus as Savior, and if you are trusting and following Him, your future looks really good!

We must not only lay all our sins down, we must leave them in the past. We must leave them there along with anything else that holds us back from trusting Him,[5] and we must surrender to the lover of our souls! He wants to have a powerful and redemptive relationship with us that affects our future lives because He loves us so much.

We often picture God as a big, grey-haired, old man sitting on a throne, just waiting to hit us with his giant hammer when we mess up. That's not God. God looks down on us with love as He yearns to have a personal relationship with us and lead us into the future—and into His work. His desire is not to punish us but to show us His great love. Why would anyone reject such a loving Father?

God not only loves us with an undying love, He has great plans for us. We may sometimes think of ourselves as weak and useless, but He looks at us and sees what He can do through us. It is far more than we could ever imagine. We often feel

---

(1 Corinthians 1:30).

5 "Therefore, since we are surrounded by such a great cloud of witnesses, let us throw off everything that hinders and the sin that so easily entangles, and let us run with perseverance the race marked out for us" (Hebrews 12:1).

worthless, but when He looks at us, He always sees us as priceless—worth giving His life to redeem. That changes everything about our future.

How do you stand today? Do you feel worthless? Do you feel like you are just taking up space here on planet earth and just *going through the motions* from day to day? Maybe it's time for you to learn the art of surrender.

That's what I had to do. I was reluctant to look beyond my failures to see my future in Christ. He had a future laid out for me, and he still does. But in order for me to begin the journey that He charted out for me, I had to surrender to the way He saw me instead of being bound by the way I saw myself. I had to learn how to surrender to His will and leave the past behind. And today I'm still learning more about the art of surrendering to my Lord.

However you feel, regardless of how black you may feel your sins are or have been, and whatever circumstance you are allowing to hold you back, just repent of it all and lay everything down at the feet of Christ. Leave your sins in the past and surrender your future to Jesus!

Let Christ take the heavy burden of sin and guilt from your shoulders and give you the peace and relief of freedom that only He can provide. Let Him show you that no matter what has happened to you in the past, or no matter what you have done in this life before today, you are still precious to Him, and He has work for you to do.

He will not stop loving you! He cares for you, and He has

wonderful plans for you. But you need to surrender to Him to realize them.

You could never make a better decision than to yield your life to God's plans. You are so loved! Now allow God to work in you and through you. Allow Him to do what He wants to do. Surrender to Him completely and allow the Lord to accomplish His will in your life.

CHAPTER 4

ANSWERING THE CALL

THE FOLLOWING PASSAGE contains instructions that Jesus gave to His disciples after His physical work on Earth was done—after His resurrection and just before His ascension. We call these instructions the Church's *Great Commission.*

> *Then the eleven disciples went to Galilee, to the mountain where Jesus had told them to go. When they saw him, they worshiped him; but some doubted. Then Jesus came to them and said, "All authority in heaven and on earth has been given to me. Therefore go and make disciples of all nations, baptizing them in the name of the Father and of the Son and of the Holy Spirit, and teaching them to obey everything I have commanded you. And surely I am with you always, to the very end of the age"*
> (Matthew 28:16-20).

Believers are still going about fulfilling the Great Commission today—nearly 2,000 years later—and this commission will remain in full force as long as there are Christians living on the face of the earth. Fulfilling the Great Commission is the Church's appointed ministry, and we should never hear Christians say they have no involvement in it.

We do not all have the same gifts and talents. We have not all been called to do the exact same things. But all of us are being called by God to be involved in the work of the Church.

If for some reason you believe you are not called as a believer into ministry to others, you are mistaken. If you are a believer, you *are* being called. And in our callings we must all realize that regardless of the types of ministries we are given, we—like the disciples of Christ who ministered before us—are called upon to fulfill the Great Commission. If our ministries revolve around another purpose, we should examine our motives and redirect our efforts.

Regardless of our experience or position, the greatest thing we can still ever do for God is to lead other people to Him and make disciples. One of the themes in my ministry is that *God is a Good Father.* As a good father, our Lord does not want anyone to perish. His love transcends all boundaries as He reaches out to both the obedient and disobedient.

God's love reaches out to everyone because we are all the children of His Creation (Christ died for all); and God is good enough, and big enough, to have purposes and plans for each and every one of us. But of course in order for God to have His way in fulfilling His plans in our lives, we must respond positively to His love as He reaches out and calls us into His service.

Hopefully you have a desire to reach out to others to share His love as you fulfill the Great Commission. The way the Bible presents things, it should only be natural for all of us who name the name of Christ to have a desire to share Him with other people. And none of us should require a special calling to share the love of Christ with anyone.

I once heard the story of a very effective missionary in another country. When he was interviewed, he was asked, "When were you called into ministry?"

He answered, "I can't remember a specific time when I was actually called. I just heard that God needed volunteers, and I went!"

There are many obvious things we can do to minister every day of our lives right where we are. We can witness by sharing our testimony with a lost friend or loved one, by helping someone in need, or just by providing someone a kind and listening ear. But what about those times when you feel like God is calling you to a specific ministry? And what about feeling like God is calling you, but you have no idea what the ministry He is calling you to even looks like?

I can certainly relate to that.

In the last chapter I wrote about a women's conference I attended, and how God called me into ministry. He doesn't always call us in such a dramatic way. And as I consider the way He called me, I sometimes think that I was so stubborn He knew His call to me would need to be very obvious if I were to hear and believe it. And after that experience, there was no doubt in my mind that He had called me.

But I wondered, "What on earth have you called me to do?"

My mind went back to the visiting pastor who came to speak at our church on that Sunday night a few years earlier. He said I was called to be an *evangelist*, and I thought he was crazy. "Could he have been right?" I thought. "No, not a chance. There is no way I could ever do that!"

As I began to ponder what God was leading me to do for Him, I decided it would be a good idea to go to every women's conference or retreat going on anywhere near me in order to find further direction. So two weeks later, some friends and I attended another conference in Des Moines. After the guest speaker had shared her message, she asked, "Would anyone like me to pray for you?"

I thought, "Here's my chance! I'll have her pray for me, and maybe God will tell her what He wants me to do for Him."

"God called me into ministry," I told her, "but I'm not sure what kind of ministry."

She prayed for me briefly. Then she looked me in the eye and said, "God says you already know what He's called you to do, so get to it!"

I left that meeting feeling more confused than before I went.

I didn't know how I was going to figure out what the Lord was calling me to do, and I was desperately looking for someone to tell me. As time passed, and that didn't happen, I began to notice that women always seemed to talk to me about all their problems. It seemed as if they were drawn to me like a magnet. Many women came to me at church and asked me to pray for them. Random strangers stopped me in stores and shared their problems. I started thinking, "Maybe God is calling me into women's ministry."

I prayed, "Jesus, if you are calling me to be a women's minister, I'm asking you to open that door for me."

I love how God answers us when we learn to pray the right kind of prayers. He didn't want me running around all over creation having others pray for me with the hope that *they* would tell me what God wanted me to do. He wanted me to come straight to Him. And when I did, He answered.

It was probably less than two weeks later that my pastor came to me and said, "I really feel like God has put this on my heart, but I want you to pray about it. I just feel that the Lord wants me to ask you to be the women's minister in our church."

I immediately said, "Yes!"

My pastor then said, "You can pray about it. You don't have to give me an answer right now."

But I already knew the answer. God had just opened the first door for me, and this was really going to happen! I was thrilled, amazed, grateful, and at the same time, scared to death.

"What on earth was I thinking?" I later asked myself. "I can't lead a women's group! I'll have to speak in front of them, and there is no way I can do that."

Fear began to creep in. I was excited about being asked, but I started doubting my abilities; and soon I was almost overcome with fear.

"Now what?" I asked myself.

Soon I was to speak for our very first ladies event. I could barely contain my excitement, but I also felt very sick in my stomach. I was so nervous. Everything that could possibly go wrong was playing over and over in my mind like a broken record. Then I started to panic over *what* to speak about. I begged God to give me a message. I pored through the Scriptures trying to find something that hit me with such impact that I would know beyond a shadow of a doubt *that* was what he wanted me to share.

I prayed and prayed, and I searched the Scriptures frantically. It was drawing very close to the event, and I was sure I was going to have a nervous breakdown. I started watching Beth Moore, Joyce Meyer, Christine Caine, and other women in ministry. They were all so good—so eloquent, educated, funny, and inspiring—and I knew I didn't match up.

At this point, I was thinking I really messed up. "God didn't call me to do this. If he had really called me to do this, it would be easy," I convinced myself. "It certainly looks easy for Beth Moore. But this is way too hard for me."

I was discouraged, disappointed, and disgusted with myself for ever thinking I could be called to this ministry.

The more I worried about it, the more I became completely overwhelmed with doubt and fear. The thought of even being able to stand before a group of people and utter a single word looked like an absolute impossibility. And the fact that I had *nothing at all to say* didn't inspire courage, either.

It was only a few days away from the event by that time, and I still had nothing! I was thinking, "There are going to be so many ladies there, and they are expecting me to have something really good to say, and I've got nothing."

In that moment it was as if God simply spoke into my heart, "I know there will be many ladies there to hear something. But remember, they are coming to hear Me speak, not you. And if they are coming to hear Me speak, do you think I will not give you—My mouthpiece—the words to say? Relax in Me, and I will provide."

I felt a little bit better about it after that . . . for a minute or two . . . but then I said, "Well, can you hurry up and give your mouthpiece a hint about what it will be saying?"

I really think God has to look at us at times and just laugh. Otherwise I think the utter frustration we cause would infuriate Him, and He would have to strike us down with lightning!

I went to bed that night exhausted—and without a message. But I woke up at about 2:00 a.m. and could not go back to sleep. Then in the stillness and quiet of the night, God began to speak to me all the things He wanted me to share. I had to get up and go write it all down. It seemed like He was pouring it into me so fast! After I had written it all down, I went back to bed and slept like a baby.

I was really surprised the next morning to find that I had not written down during the night a bunch of meaningless mumbo-jumbo that didn't make any sense. The message was clear, and all the corresponding Bible verses began to click in my mind. After adding the final touches and praying over the message, I had to apologize to God for getting so distraught and doubting Him.

We need to consider that if God has called us to do something, He will provide what we need to do it. The Lord is looking for workers; He will give us the tools. I wasn't able to come up with anything that I felt was *good enough* in my own power. But God stepped in—in his timing—to give me the words that He had for me to deliver to His daughters.

The day came for me to deliver my message, and I was still nervous as I entered the church. I had to go to the restroom and talk-myself-up at least three times before I took the platform. But guess what happened? The Holy Spirit took over as soon as I began to speak. The anointing swept in, and I felt like I had been doing that type of ministry all my life. Don't get me wrong, I knew I had a long way to go, but wherever I was going, I also knew I was not going alone.

God was right there with me, and the Holy Spirit was leading me. I learned that I just needed to be obedient and let Him use me—let Him speak through me.

Sometimes God calls us to do the very things that seem impossible for us—things scary or unbelievable for us to accomplish. But I can confidently tell you that no matter what God is calling you to do, He has the ability to do it through you.

We must not limit ourselves by what we can or cannot do through our own abilities. He sees far more potential in us than we can ever see in ourselves.

After that meeting, I don't know if my feet even touched the floor on my way out of the building. I think I literally floated out to my car. Many women approached me and said, "I had no idea you could speak like that."

I told them, "You were not as surprised as I was, because I didn't know I could either."

I was so overwhelmed by what God did. I was finally starting to see through the dark veil of the impossible, and I was beginning to realize the things that had seemed so unreachable might actually be attainable after all.

At a recent speaking engagement God revealed to me that He was calling a specific individual to be an evangelist. He was a complete stranger, and I knew absolutely nothing about him. When I shared with him what God had shown me, he began to cry. He said, "I used to think He called me. I even went to Bible school, and graduated. But I have been so overcome with fear and doubt that I finally gave up."

He then looked at me and said, "I just want to know for sure. You are so confident and have no doubts. I don't want to have any doubts. You know exactly what God has called you to do, and you don't hesitate to do it. I want to be just like that."

I said, "Good luck with that one!"

I began to share with him that I always have doubts. I said, "I still face fears. So many times I feel ill-equipped to do what God asks me to do. But if I let the fear and doubt win, I wouldn't be doing what I am doing today. It doesn't matter how many times we do something or see God do amazing things through it, we may still sometimes deal with doubts. Doubt does not have to be a bad thing if we keep it in the right perspective."

You see, doubt should simply remind us of the weaknesses and shortcomings that continue to exist in us—and will certainly be on display if we attempt to perform our callings in our own power. Our doubt should not stop us from doing God's work; it should drive us to dependency on God and His power.

I can truthfully say that I doubt my own abilities every day. But I know my heavenly Father can do anything He wants—whatever He decides to do. To me, my own abilities have absolutely nothing to do with what God decides to accomplish through me. However, my obedience has everything to do with it. And obedience is the key to overcoming our doubts and fears when it comes to answering God's call to ministry.

I absolutely believe God has called me to speak and minister. But I hope I always retain some degree of doubt and reservations about my abilities. I pray that God always keeps me humble and never allows me to get in His way. I don't want to be overconfident. I am completely honest in saying that I put no confidence in myself, but I put all the confidence imaginable in my Savior. I doubt my abilities, but I don't doubt His.

If we wait until we *feel* confident, or if we wait until we have absolutely *no doubts* about what he has called us to do, then we will probably never realize the calling He has given us. When we answer the call that God has placed on our lives, we may still have some doubts and be tempted to fear; but Jesus walks with us through all of them.

When we are seeking to follow Christ wholeheartedly, in total surrender and obedience, He will lead us into some of the most amazing adventures as we join the rest of the Church in fulfilling the Great Commission. But we must step out in faith and obedience.

Dear Christian, you must answer the call God has placed on your life before you will experience the adventure He has planned for you.

CHAPTER 5

JEALOUSY

SEVERAL YEARS AGO I was struggling and praying to receive the perfect message from God for an upcoming speaking engagement. Unfortunately, I was feeling absolutely no direction whatsoever. It seemed that God was being completely silent. The date of my speaking commitment was nearing, and I was almost in a state of panic.

Once again I was tempted to doubt and despair.

I thought, "Can I even do this?" Immediately I began to think about others who I believed were better speakers, funnier, more in-depth, better equipped, taller, thinner, prettier, and more eloquent than I; and I was almost ready to throw in the towel.

"God, please give me something to say to them!" I pleaded.

Finally, in exhaustion I went to bed without a message. I will never forget what happened next. That evening as I lay in bed, God provided a message to me that I would not soon forget. Just before falling asleep, I began to think about my childhood; and one very funny memory sprang to mind.

I remembered how at Christmas my brother and I were always so excited to open our gifts. We would sit down in front of the Christmas tree, and our mom and dad would pass our presents to us. I would rip into mine with eager anticipation, thrilled to see what the festive colored packages contained.

My brother would sit and watch me. After I opened a gift, he would ask my parents, "How much did that cost?" When I opened the next one, he would look at my parents and ask, "How much did you pay for that one?" It was so frustrating! He would sit there and count up how much money they had spent on me so he would know if they paid more for my presents than his.

My parents were always very fair, and they always treated us equally when it came to gifts. Every year our gifts totaled the same amount; yet my brother would sit there surrounded by his gifts and watch me open mine. He was sure I was going to receive something more expensive or exciting than what he received. Finally, my parents were so exasperated that they just began to leave the price tags on everything in hope of putting a stop to his asking.

I started thinking about how silly it was for my brother to sit there and miss the fun of opening his gifts because he was so preoccupied with what I was getting. He could be enjoying his own gifts if he weren't so busy watching me open mine!

I chuckled to myself as I sat in bed recounting this childhood memory, but then God spoke to my heart. He simply whispered to me, "That's exactly what My children do. I have given you all so many gifts, perfectly suited to each one alone. But you are busy worrying about a gift someone else has, and whether it is better than yours, rather than opening the gifts I have given to you."

That reality pierced my heart like an arrow! I was guilty of sitting there surrounded by my own unopened gifts while watching others to see if their gifts were better than mine.

How many times are we guilty of putting price tags on our gifts so we can compare them to the gifts others receive? God is fair and just. And regardless of how we may be tempted to esteem or rank the gifts He has given to each of us, they are all valuable; and the Lord needs each and every one of us to use our own special gifts to accomplish His will and purpose.

That night I was reminded of the need to stop comparing myself to others and open my own gifts. He has given to each one of us the gifts perfectly suited to us.

In his grace, God has given us different gifts for doing certain things well. So if God has given you the ability to prophesy, speak out with as much faith as God has given you. If your gift is serving others, serve them well. If you are a teacher, teach well. If your gift is to encourage others, be encouraging. If it is giving, give generously. If God has given you leadership ability, take the responsibility seriously. And if you have a gift for showing kindness to others, do it gladly.

(Romans 12:6-9 NLT)

So, why do people so often feel the need to compare themselves to others? And considering the primary audience of this book, why do we women so often compare ourselves and our gifts to other women? Could it be that we are struggling with jealousy? I'm afraid that jealousy is often, if not always, the case.

When we start comparing ourselves to others and begin ranking the perceived value of the gifts we possess, we can start criticizing ourselves based on what we see in the talents and abilities of others instead of maintaining a healthy focus on how our own lives meet God's expectations. Then, if we're not careful, we become afraid that if, for instance, someone comes along who sings prettier or speaks more eloquently, others will like us less, and we will lose our rightful place in their esteem. But whose esteem do we value the most—God's esteem or the esteem of other people?

When we get caught up in such comparisons, we can lose sight of the fact that our gifts, talents, physical appearance, and other attributes, are not the only things that make us who we are. Our existence and value go beyond these things—and they must.

If we pride and define ourselves as being the best singers compared to others who sing, and we lose our voices, who are we then? If each of us were stripped down to a white T-shirt and a pair of black leggings, with no make-up and—God forbid—no hair products, jewelry, or talents, how would we view ourselves then? Would we still be "enough?" And enough for whom? Enough for us? Enough for God?

The truth is, if we judge ourselves as being *not enough* without our stuff, we will also never be enough with it.

When we take away everything we *think* we are, what's left? Hopefully there will always be something to respect about us beyond our physical attributes, material possessions, and talents. What does our *inner man* look like? Of course we can't literally see inside us, but what qualities do we radiate when there is nothing left but what we think is a shell of ourselves? Does any beauty remain? Are we reflecting the image of our Father in Heaven? Or is our image defiled by the ugly, twisted appearance of jealousy, bitterness, and envy?

Jealousy and envy in our lives, like bitter weeds if allowed to grow, can quickly take over the remaining, beautiful, and wholesome parts of us and choke them out.

Look after each other so that none of you fails to receive the grace of God. Watch out that no poisonous root of bitterness grows up to trouble you, corrupting many.

(Hebrews 12:15 NLT)

Jealousy is a bitter poison. It often proves to be one of the most destructive forces we face. And since jealousy is no respecter of persons, there is no one who hasn't felt a tinge of jealousy at some point in his or her life.

For sure, there is always some kind of kindling at the core of a fire. And when it comes to jealousy, you can be sure that our spiritual enemy is waiting and watching for the first opportunity he has to throw some fuel on it and drop a match. He knows that a blaze of jealousy could burn over most anything.

The devil knows jealousy causes division. He knows that if he can convince us to focus on what someone else has, and influence us to compare those things to what we have, he will have his dirty old foot in the doorway of our hearts.

Jealousy can grow in us like cancer. It steals people's joy, and makes them bitter. It robs people of valuable relationships and friendships, and it puts a wedge between them and God. It begins to consume their every thought. It oozes out of every pore in the form of negativity, and it often leads to acts of disobedience.

We must be careful to never let jealousy take root and start to grow. We must learn to respect ourselves as God's people and see ourselves the way God sees us. And if we find even a hint of jealousy in our lives or being exhibited toward us by someone else, we should immediately repent of any jealousy we harbor or start praying for the person who is jealous of us.

It's hard to dislike people you are praying for. Our compassion grows toward them, and we are then able to love them like God loves us. In turn we will begin to value how our differences can be used by God to do more, instead of seeing them as a threat.

Before God called me into ministry I had a dear friend in a leadership position. She had a wealth of knowledge about ministry and a ton of experience to go along with it. As I told you earlier, my pastor asked me to be the women's leader at our church, and I knew it was definitely a "God thing." I had been praying for God to open a door and help me have the faith to step through it when the time came. He soon flung the door wide open, and when He did, I gladly accepted the position.

The very first time I stood before that group of ladies to minister to them, I was completely overwhelmed by the power and presence of God in that room. I knew He was confirming His calling on my life, because that was *not me*! I had always been an introvert, shy, and quiet. But as I began to speak the words He gave me, a boldness like I had never known sprang up within me.

I was beyond elated when the service was over. All the ladies gathered around me after the event to tell me how much they enjoyed it, and I was totally overwhelmed by their kind words. That is, all the ladies except for one.

My dear sweet friend—the one whose opinion I valued the most—was avoiding me. She eventually told me before I left that I did a good job, but there was a hint of coldness in her tone. Her whole demeanor toward me seemed to have changed. I hoped it was my imagination, and I told myself that she was probably tired or preoccupied. But, somehow I still sensed a problem. Something in her demeanor had stiffened, and she was different.

As time passed, God continued to do amazing things in my life and ministry. I was continually overwhelmed and amazed by the doors of opportunity that He continued to swing open. But, I noticed that my friend was becoming more and more distant. I tried to include her in everything, and I invited her to special events and engagements that I was invited to, but she never wanted to go. Still, she insisted that I call her when I returned home from them to let her know how things went.

I called to share my ecstatic news with her after one particularly exciting event, and she seemed to be happy for me. However, the next day at church she wouldn't even speak to me. I knew something was definitely bothering her.

I called her the next day and asked her to tell me what she was upset about. For a while she denied anything was wrong. Finally, she told me she was jealous of me. I was stunned. This lady was a friend whom I admired. She was strong in leadership skills and talented far beyond any talent I possessed. I couldn't figure out why she would feel jealous.

She shared that she had tried to get past it, but she was still struggling with it. I felt horrible. I wanted to help her so she wouldn't feel that way. I prayed for her right then and there. Still, I knew it had put a wedge between us.

Now that I knew how she felt, I no longer wanted to tell her any of the exciting things God was doing in my life. I didn't want her to be jealous. I was afraid she might think I was bragging, and I certainly didn't want to do anything to make her feel worse. I even began to point out and compliment her on her talents and other strong points.

Although I prayed for her on a regular basis, I could still detect a feeling of awkwardness between us. The air was always heavy with tension when we were in a room together. And it was affecting my ability to minister to our ladies group because

I knew what she was feeling toward me as I stood before them. I considered that a huge loss; for I needed her not only as a friend but also as a mentor, and she would have been such a good one for me with all of her former experience.

I was completely at my wit's end. I didn't know what else to do. I had asked her to help me with the women's group and had included her in all the decisions. I had also given her great recognition as a leader. I had prayed for her until I felt I was completely out of breath, and the situation seemed to only worsen.

Our ladies group had grown and seemed to be flourishing. It seemed like a most unlikely time for me to throw in the towel, but I was smothered beneath such a weight of bondage every time I attempted to hold a meeting! Soon, I began to pray to God for a new direction.

I asked the Lord to show me what to do in the situation. I knew that He understood my friend's heart, and God alone knew if she would be able to overcome the jealousy, and whether or not we would be able to salvage our relationship. It was clear that my friend wanted the position as the women's minister for herself. And I felt like God was leading me and my family to leave the church.

I didn't want to leave the church, though, because I loved all the people there. We had been there for several years, and they had become our *family*. But I still felt the Lord urging me to leave.

I can be quite stubborn and hard to convince, so I asked the Lord to close the door that He had earlier opened for me if He really wanted us to leave. Within two weeks I received a phone call to tell me that both Men's and Women's Ministries were going to be shut down because we would soon be starting a small groups ministry. I was heartbroken, but I knew that was my undeniable answer.

We spoke to our pastors, and told them we were not upset or angry with anyone, but we knew God was leading us away. We left the "right way." We said goodbye to the congregation, and they sent us off with their prayers and blessings. My friend and I hugged, and cried. I think we both knew deep down that this was the end of the road for our close-knit friendship. As painful as it was, this had become the only solution.

Only a couple of weeks had passed when I heard that my friend was leading a women's Sunday school group. I wasn't surprised at all. It was a shame that the situation had to be resolved in such a manner. But we still kept in touch, and we remained friends until the miles separated us indefinitely.

Truly, God always has a plan. He immediately led us into a larger church where He opened the door for me to serve as the women's minister for a much larger group of women. These women very quickly became my "new cherished family!" The Lord also gave me the mentor I desperately needed and continued to teach me. He showed me how to handle all kinds of difficult relationships.

We all can have and deal with so many issues, but the most destructive one I have experienced was when the enemy found a way to drive a wedge between God's children with the poison of jealousy. Be on guard. Love one another, pray for each other, and when the first sprout of jealousy rears its ugly head, chop it off.

Jealousy causes disorder in God's house. There's no room for it in the life of a daughter of the King.

The entire law is summed up in keeping this one command: "Love your neighbor as yourself." If you bite and devour each other, watch out or you will be destroyed by each other.

(Galatians 5:14-15)

For where you have envy and selfish ambition, there you find disorder and every evil practice. (James 3:16)

CHAPTER 6

FOR REASONS AND SEASONS

WHEN GOD CALLS someone into ministry (regardless of the type of ministry), He knows the person He is calling needs to be equipped for that work. As we reach out to touch the lives of others, we certainly need the spiritual equipment God supplies. We need to be equipped with God's anointing and direction.[6] And without doubt, we all need the Holy Spirit's empowerment in order to do the Lord's work.

It also helps so much to receive the encouragement and support of friends. I have been blessed by enduring friendships with some fellow-believers who have become long-term members of my support team, and I don't know what I would do without them.

In addition to those special, close friends and supporters, though, I also have been blessed over the years to have other friends in whose lives I've had shorter periods of personal

---

6   And don't forget to put on the armor of God mentioned in
    Ephesians 6:10-18.

involvement. I have benefitted from having some wonderful, valuable relationships with them even though our active contact lasted only a short time.

I say without hesitation that regardless of how long we have been involved in each other's lives, all my friends have been used by God to enrich my life and ministry.

But when it comes to talking about relationships with people who have been used by God to improve my life and ministry, I also can say that some of those relationships have been with people who were not only *not* friends, they were people who openly opposed me. But I give glory to God for having led me through both the good and not-so-good relationships that I've had with people during my ministry. God enabled even people who opposed me to contribute to my success as a minister in ways they may never understand.

God will purposely bring godly people into our lives to be our friends, bless us with support, and provide us with opportunities for Christian growth. But He will also allow some people who are not supportive to cross our paths in order to challenge us and help us grow and mature in our ability to minister God's love to others. Our relationships with those who oppose us may not be too enjoyable, but our experiences with them will be used by God to bring about our spiritual growth and teach us lessons that we could learn no other way.

The Lord is active in every season of our lives and ministries; and in His wisdom, God always has good reasons to do the things He does when He brings people into our lives. Through all these relationships, we can be confident that He is continuing to certify our callings and improve our abilities to represent Him.

Years ago, when my husband and I started attending a local church in Davenport Iowa, God brought me into contact with some people who became very dear friends. The pastor, Scott Rooks, immediately welcomed us with open arms. Although he did not know me really well, he took a chance on me—first inviting me to speak for a women's brunch, and then asking me to lead the church's women's ministry.

And I instantly hit it off with Ann, the pastor's wife. We had so much in common; and with both of us having a similar sense of humor, there was never a dull moment any time we were together. We sometimes shared deep personal issues with one another, but we also enjoyed many fun and lighthearted conversations. We soon became best friends, and in just a short period of time I felt as though I had known Pastor Scott and Ann all my life.

I was working toward getting my ministerial credentials when I first joined the church, so it was an awkward period of transition for me. I hesitantly asked Pastor Scott to be my mentor, even though we had only known each other for maybe a month. But he agreed, and I soon realized that God had purposely brought me to that church and under the leadership of its pastor. Pastor Scott mentored me with patience and an honest desire to help me succeed.

I couldn't begin to list all the reasons why I believe he was a great example for me as a young minister. Pastor Scott spent time with me discussing all kinds of questions I had about ministry. He helped me understand the ups and downs of Christian ministry, and he showed me that my greatest calling was to always be obedient to Christ—even when it wasn't the popular thing to do. I received my certificate of ministry from the Assemblies of God under his mentorship, and what I feel is a lifelong partnership was built between us in praying for and encouraging one another.

Some of the people whom I have chosen for friends over the years, though, have not worked out nearly so well. I have had individuals show up and appear to be friends who were devoted to me only to find out later that they had ulterior motives. Instead of speaking encouragement into my life, they ended up bringing me discouragement.

Some people have even pretended to be friends in order to try to get information about me that could be used against me for their own benefit. Others were genuine friends until jealousy or some other influence of the enemy drove them away. Some remained friends with me only as long as they could get something of monetary or material value from me.

Even though these were not true or lasting friends, I believe God allowed all of them to be a part of my life for good reason; for I have learned from my experiences with each of them. You know, God is always teaching us through our experiences in life. If only we would be better learners!

In many cases, false friends, and friends who have later forsaken me, have revealed to me the kind of person I did not want to become. They showed me how hurtful people can be—sometimes without even realizing it. Some served as living examples of how sin and mistakes in our lives can lead to destruction.

Through all of those painful relationships, I learned more about how to value others, and how to be extra careful about not hurting people like I had been hurt. Some lessons are not easily learned without having them really driven home in a dramatic way; and I'm thankful for the things God has taught me by leading me through those experiences.

Thankfully, the true, lasting, and faithful friendships I have formed with others have more than made up for all the relationships that were painful. Those trusted friends have been great teachers, mentors, and encouragers. They have spoken godly wisdom into my life and shared ministry experiences with me. Thank God for all of them. Whether or not they recognize it, I see them as having been on (or still being on) a mission from God to help equip and prepare me for His service.

But not all of them were meant to stay connected to me or my ministry for a long period of time. God sent some of them along for only a short season in my life to help Him accomplish a work that needed to be done in me at the time—to guide me, teach me a lesson, or increase my understanding.

God led some into my life who were going through the same problems I was going through. God sent them to me so I might realize I was not alone in my struggles—or just so we could help each other sort things out in our lives. They had special insight into my situation; and because of that, we could support and agree with one another in prayer with special understanding.

Yes, there have been many friends whom I count dear who were only meant to be in my life for a season. But there was always a good reason for the fellowship that developed between us. In our Christian discipleship, we need to develop true and faithful friends—not only for our own benefit but also for the benefit of others. Just because some of our friendships don't last a lifetime, or even years, that doesn't necessarily mean our friendships were failures or did not fulfill their purposes.

When we lose contact or frequent fellowship with someone whom we counted as a friend, it may just mean that God has a new friend for us. When you experience that, look for God to bring someone else into your life for yet another reason—even if it is, again, only for a season.

But God also sends *us* out to be friends with others. Look for those opportunities. God wants you to be someone's friend—and likely a friend to many. The Lord has a reason for you to meet that person, and He has something for you to accomplish that will bring value to that person's life. People may need you as a friend for life; or they may need your friendship only for a time. But always remember that they definitely need you. Be a friend in need. Be a friend indeed.

Being in ministry, I come into contact with a lot of people. I love meeting God's wonderful children. Every time I go to speak at a church, a women's conference, or some other special event, I meet women who just pour out their hearts to me. I pray with them, and it's just an amazing experience.

I love all of my sisters-in-Christ with whom I come into contact. I know that God has put me into their lives. And I want to be their friend, even if only for a short time. My heart yearns to build long-lasting friendships with each one of them, but that isn't always possible. (Of course, many of the wonderful ladies I meet add me as their friend on social media, so I do actually have an opportunity to stay in touch with some of them that way.)

It is just not humanly possible to have a deep-rooted, personal friendship with each one of the people to whom I minister. There are just too many of them, and there are still only 24 hours in a day. I have come to realize that, in most cases, God has sent me to them to be their friend for only a moment—to minister to a need, to encourage, or to give godly advice—and then to move on.

If I have done my part in being God's messenger—being His hands and feet on Earth—I depart from them knowing that I am leaving them in relationship with, and in the hands of, another friend who will never leave them or forsake them.[7] God is the best friend to whom we can point people. He is our friend not only for a season, nor only for a lifetime, but forever.

People are sometimes sent directly to us by God to be our friends, but as I referred to earlier, there are also others, who seemingly come only to oppose or torment us—who, while not being sent or inspired by God, are still allowed by Him in His wisdom to become part of our lives. I'm talking about people who

---

7 "Be strong and courageous. Do not be afraid or terrified because of them, for the Lord your God goes with you; he will never leave you nor forsake you" (Deuteronomy 31:6). See also Hebrews 13:5.

may even appear to be friends, but who are not motivated by God to do us any favors or further His kingdom. God may sometimes allow such people to enter our lives and affect our ministries because He plans to turn their disruptions around for our good.

There was a lady who showed up in a women's group I was leading and represented herself immediately as a friend and supporter. We had talked and shared with each other, and had a decent relationship while we had been involved together in other church functions. But not long after starting to attend the women's group under my leadership, she started to act quite differently. It was like she took off her mask to reveal who she really was.

She began behaving like she was out to hinder the women's ministry in any way she could. Many times she would start talking and try to take over a meeting. After a time it became clear to me that she was trying to assert authority over me and make me feel like I was incapable of doing what God called me to do.

I was forced to quickly develop some leadership skills that allowed me to deal with her in a delicate way but not allow her to hinder what God was trying to do in the lives of the other women. But soon she began to attack other women in the group as well. She was trying to cause discord among us, and she was purposefully hurting people with her harsh words.

Besides leading the women's ministry at our church, I also held a weekly home Bible study for women in my neighborhood. When she found out about the Bible study, she asked if she could join us. I couldn't refuse, so I reluctantly allowed her to join the study group.

The first few weeks with her in attendance in the Bible study went fine, but one day it was like someone had flipped a switch, and she started twisting around the words I was speaking and accusing me of directing negative words at her. I was in complete shock—as were the others in attendance—as she began yelling and screaming at me.

The other ladies tried to tell her that I did not say what she was implying; and I repeatedly tried to apologize, even though I knew I had done nothing wrong. But she continued yelling and hurling insults at me. She then grabbed her purse and went out the door, slamming it behind her. The rest of us were left sitting there in shock and wondering what had just happened.

A couple of weeks later, I took the church's women's group to a large women's conference. The *great disrupter* (as I thought of her) went with us, of course. She had already tried to start an argument with the bus driver on the way to the conference, and she wouldn't speak to anyone. I knew she was a ticking time bomb. But the more I tried to defuse the situation, the more volatile it seemed to become.

Eventually, she grabbed my arm, pulled me aside, and began to blatantly lie to me about the bus driver. She was telling me all kinds of things that I knew were simply not true. I told her, "This is not the time or place to discuss the matter; we can talk about it when we all get home."

Then she followed me into the auditorium and began screaming at me to the top of her lungs, "You are not fit to be a women's minister! God will never use you. You were never called to do this. You are a pitiful excuse for a minister!"

It seemed to me like everyone in the entire auditorium was looking at us.

I was almost speechless . . . almost. For it was in that moment when I felt God's power envelop me as I calmly and quietly said to her, "You may not think that God has called me to be a minister, but I know exactly what He has called me to do. I also know that I am the one whom God has put into this position, at this time, and you will not ruin this trip and this weekend for the ladies who are here to seek and worship God."

She quickly spun around and left the auditorium. When she came back she was quiet and did not cause any more trouble at the conference.

I had tried countless times to make peace between us— and between her and other ladies in the group—but she was determined to stir up confusion and conflict. She was a real *thorn in my side*. She continued to oppose me after the conference by sending me hate mail. She continued to tell me what a lousy job I was doing, and that I should sit down and shut up. She even sent me an email at one point using cursing to degrade me.

I was continually upset about one thing or another that she was doing. But in all that chaos, and through that relationship, I learned some things. First of all, God used the situation at the conference to teach me how and when to assert authority—and how to do it in a godly manner. In prior situations I would have kept quiet and hoped the whole situation would blow over. But when she started screaming at me, something welled up inside me that I had not experienced before.

I came to realize that I didn't respond to her like that because I felt sorry for myself for being insulted; instead, I did it because I felt an immense responsibility to the ladies I had taken to the conference. They did not deserve to have their entire weekend ruined because of one unruly person. I had to do something. For the first time in my eyes, the women's group actually became my flock. I had to protect them. So my generally quiet and timid nature was left behind as I corrected her in boldness and authority.

I think my response shocked me just as much as it shocked her. But that stand stopped her plotting and scheming that day, and the rest of the ladies were finally able to get something from God that weekend.

I also learned a big lesson on forgiveness. She was very difficult to love with all her hate mail and constant troublemaking, but I came to realize that she was hurting others because she herself was hurting on the inside. I began praying for her more and more fervently. And as I prayed for her, I was able to look past her actions and love her soul.

I wish I could tell you that my prayers were answered to the point that she repented, straightened out, and became a true friend to both me and the other ladies; but that didn't happen. She eventually left our fellowship and started causing trouble in another church. Though I was more than willing to be her friend—and a true friend in need and ministry—she would not allow it.

That season with her taught me many lessons.

Try to look for the lessons God is teaching you through both people who come and remain engaged in your life and those who come and go. There is always something to be gained from all the friendships and other relationships that come our way. Don't let the hurts and discouragement you experience in some relationships keep you from making new friends or stop you from ministering to those in spiritual need. Even short-term relationships and ministry opportunities can yield long-lasting, positive results.

As we go out and minister to others, we will meet all kinds of people who are experiencing all kinds of life's situations. The lessons God teaches us through our experiences with all of them are priceless. May others say the same thing about the value of our actions as we are used to minister in their own seasons of life, and may the reasons for our ministry always be motivated by God.

CHAPTER 7

FORGIVENESS

WHEN I LIVED in Iowa, I drove my children to and from a private school every day. And each day, at almost the same spot, I crossed paths with a public school bus. Like clockwork, I knew where the bus driver would stop the bus, and I always stopped well in advance of when she turned on the bus's flashing amber lights—which of course was followed by her extending the so-familiar stop sign mounted on the bus. Imagine my surprise one day when a deputy showed up on the front doorstep of my home and informed me that I had been accused of running the bus's stop sign!

At first I was in shock; I tried to recall any moment when I could have made such an error that would have put children in danger. "No!" I said. "I always stopped for that bus!"

The deputy asked me, "Were you in that area on that date?"

"Well . . . yes," I replied, "I drive that route every day taking my kids to and from school."

He then informed me I would have to pay a $700 fine and appear in court.

"What? But I didn't do it," I explained.

Soon after that, I found myself in a courtroom being sworn in before a judge. I began to state my case:

"Your honor," I said, "I am a safe driver. I've never been accused of any other serious traffic violations. And I'm a mom who adores children; I would never intentionally endanger a child. I am even a credentialed minister with the Assemblies of God. But, most importantly, I didn't do it. Why would I, a minister, lie about such a thing?"

After I'd stated my case, the bus driver took the stand. I sat there—the accused before her accuser—and listened as the bus driver made her case. First, she was asked to describe my car. She stated that it was a blue SUV.

That was completely wrong. I drove a brown Chevy Malibu. She couldn't recall any of the details about how I "ran her stop sign." She couldn't even remember the time, place, or date. After hearing all the evidence she had to offer, I was pleased with the outcome of her testimony.

Logically, I was sure this case would have to be thrown out since the bus driver didn't even know the make, model, or color of the car I drove.

You can imagine my shock when sometime after that day I received a document in the mail that stated, in part:

You have been found guilty. Your license is suspended for 30 days, after which time you will have to pay a license recovery fee. You must purchase additional insurance at a rate of $200 more per month and carry this insurance for the next 2 years. Furthermore, if pulled over at any time, for any reason within the next year, you will automatically lose your license for another 30 days, with a two-year probation period.

"Where is the justice in this?" I complained.

I was told I could appeal my case, and I determined to do so. But when I appealed, I was informed once again that I was guilty. The court's position? The bus driver had no reason to lie.

"Really? This isn't fair," I protested to myself as I stewed on the decision. "What about my rights?"

It feels horrible to be falsely accused. I felt as if the whole world was pointing at me, and saying, "You are a criminal!" For weeks I had nightmares about the courtroom with people snarling at me, repeating, "Guilty, guilty, guilty!"

But as I thought it through, I remembered someone who stood in my defense. That deputy sheriff who came to my door was in court with me, and he also took the stand.

He said, "I have no reason to believe that Mrs. Sparks ran the stop sign. I feel the bus driver is mistaken in this situation, especially considering she doesn't even know the color or model of Mrs. Sparks' car, time, day, or location. I am also highly suspicious of the fact that 17 other people also ran her stop sign this month. I believe Mrs. Sparks is innocent."

Innocent! Yes, someone believed me! I can't tell you how wonderful it felt to know that someone else in the courtroom believed I was innocent.

I can however tell you that as time progressed, my feelings toward that bus driver were anything but *warm and fuzzy*. In the many days that followed, I had to pray very hard for God to help me forgive her. And I admit that I had to pray hard because I simply didn't want to forgive her.

But God gently reminded me during that time that Satan is known as an accuser.[8] He has a surreptitious way of influencing people, and that influence can often be found in the events and issues that come our way and negatively affect us.

Then as I went over the events in my mind, I continued to think about the young deputy in the courtroom. He couldn't do anything to help me. His testimony was discounted by the judge just as mine was. But the fact that he tried to help me, and the fact that he believed I was innocent, meant the world to me. Someone was willing to question the accusations and look at the facts. The officer didn't automatically assume the worst of me, and as I decided then, he in effect extended grace to me.

---

8 "Then I heard a loud voice in heaven say: 'Now have come the salvation and the power and the kingdom of our God, and the authority of his Messiah. For the accuser of our brothers and sisters, who accuses them before our God day and night, has been hurled down. They triumphed over him by the blood of the Lamb and by the word of their testimony; they did not love their lives so much as to shrink from death. Therefore rejoice, you heavens and you who dwell in them! But woe to the earth and the sea, because the devil has gone down to you! He is filled with fury, because he knows that his time is short'" (Revelation 12:10-12).

That made me think about how I depended on God's Grace, and how He provided advocacy for us!

You see, we have an advocate who is far greater than any human who could ever represent us before a judge.[9] His name is Jesus. Jesus sees all, and He knows all. He knows when we are falsely accused. He knows when others do things to hurt us. He knows when others do harm to us or our loved ones. He knows and sees when others are rude or cruel to us, and He also knows personally the emotional pain of being misrepresented and mistreated.

But beyond the fact that we have a Savior in heaven representing us before God's throne, we also have the Holy Spirit with us here on earth to be our helper, our comforter, advocate, and counselor.[10]

When I consider the injustices of life, I'm reminded of a story in Scripture, in which the accusation of sin played a pretty big role in determining someone's trouble. I think about the woman

---

9 "Earth, do not cover my blood; may my cry never be laid to rest! Even now my witness is in heaven; my advocate is on high. My intercessor is my friend as my eyes pour out tears to God; on behalf of a man he pleads with God as a man pleads for his friend" (Job 16:18-21).

10 "And I will ask the Father, and he will give you another advocate to help you and be with you forever—the Spirit of truth." (John 14:16-17a).

"But the Advocate, the Holy Spirit, whom the Father will send in my name, will teach you all things and will remind you of everything I have said to you" (John 14:26).

In John 14:26, the Holy Spirit is spoken of as "comforter" in the KJV and American Standard Version of the Bible. He is spoken of as "advocate" (as in a legal representative or counselor) in the NIV and NLT. The NIV 1984 version uses the word "counselor." The New King James Version and New American Standard Bible use the word "Helper."

caught in adultery, and how her accusers brought her to Jesus to get Him to pronounce upon her the punishment of death by stoning (the legal remedy for her sin). Of course, unlike in my case—in my *brush with the law*—that woman *was* indeed guilty, and Jesus already knew that.

But Jesus also knew the hypocrisy of her accusers, and how they intended to use the circumstance to embarrass and discredit the Lord. So Jesus turned the issue around against her accusers and chose to forgive her. Exhibiting great wisdom and understanding, Jesus told her corrupt accusers, *"Let any one of you who is without sin be the first to throw a stone at her"* (John 8:7b).

They all dropped the stones they held in their hands and left; then Jesus asked the woman, *"Where are they? Has no one condemned you?"* (John 8:10b).

Jesus became that woman's advocate that day—both on earth and in heaven—as He gave her an opportunity to be forgiven and receive her redeemer.

Forgiveness and redemption also must be *our* themes as we go through life and attempt to fulfill the Lord's calling that He has placed on our lives. So when we find ourselves under the fire of accusations, we must seek to forgive. Our ability to extend grace and love to those who point fingers of accusation at us with the intention of hurting or harming us—or for any other reason—will bear witness to our love for Christ and the character He demonstrated in the story of the woman caught in adultery as recorded in John chapter eight.

Still, it was very hard for me to forgive the bus driver who had caused all kinds of inconveniences for me—and cost me a lot of money. I really wanted to give her a piece of my mind, but I knew it was my place to forgive. I knew God wanted me to respond by forgiving her.

When we have been wronged by someone, praying for that person is sometimes the last thing we want to do. But for us to be able to forgive and find peace in our struggles, that's exactly what we *must* do.

So I prayed. I first prayed that God would give me compassion for the bus driver and help me to love her. I've learned through several experiences in life that it is not only hard to pray for people who have wronged us, it is also hard to genuinely love them. And it is extremely hard to love someone when our emotions are moving us toward the opposite.

Therefore, my first prayer was to ask the Lord to give me compassion because I knew God wanted me to exhibit His love. As I continued to pray that prayer, I began to wonder what the bus driver's life looked like. Through my ordeal I eventually found out that she accused many people every month of running her bus's stop sign. The deputy eventually told me she had done it so often that they were secretly investigating her by following her along her route in an unmarked car. Unfortunately for me, though, that was information he could not divulge in court.

"What could possibly make a person so unhappy," I wondered. "What would cause her to continually lie about other people?"

I knew she needed help, so I then began to pray for her spiritual condition. I had no idea what her beliefs were, but I prayed that God would begin to reveal himself to her as a loving Father.

I continued to pray prayers focused on the healing of her heart, and as I prayed, I began to have peace in *mine*. My anger toward her began to diminish, and I started to thank God that I have the privilege of knowing Him as Father. I didn't know how to contact that lady bus driver, but I always prayed that if I had the opportunity to meet her in a store or some other location, God would give me the chance to share His love with her.

A few months later I heard that she was no longer working for the school, and I never saw her again.

There will always be people who do things that we don't like. There will be some who will do horrible things or say terrible things about us. When that happens, we must forgive them. We must forgive them if we intend to maintain a healthy relationship with our Lord, who every day forgives people who wrong Him. We must forgive them for our own benefit. You see, when it comes right down to it, our acts of forgiving others benefit *us*.

Even if the people we forgive are not changed or moved toward God, His work will continue to grow in us more and more as we reflect His nature by forgiving others.

And remember this principle: We must forgive if we want to be forgiven.

"And when you stand praying, if you hold anything against anyone, forgive them, so that your Father in heaven may forgive you your sins." (Mark 11:25)

"For if you forgive other people when they sin against you, your heavenly Father will also forgive you. But if you do not forgive others their sins, your Father will not forgive your sins." (Matthew 6:14-15)

Forgiving those who wrong you may be difficult, but as you strive to become more like Christ, you will learn to forgive as He forgave. We learn to forgive others as we increase our appreciation for the fact that He forgave—and continues to forgive—us.

I'm reminded of an episode on the television show, *American Idol*. Some years ago a woman named Mandisa appeared on the show. When she walked into the room to audition for the judges—with millions of people all over the nation tuned into the program—one of the judges, Simon Cowell, smirked and said, "Do we have a bigger stage this year?"

Mandisa had always struggled with her weight, and his comment hurt her deeply since she was very overweight at the time. After her audition, the TV producers and directors told her to let him have it when she went back out to face him. They told her not to worry about her language because they could bleep it out.

She walked back out there and said this: "Yes, you hurt me. And I cried. And it was painful. It really was. But I want you to know that I have forgiven you, and that you don't need someone to apologize in order to forgive somebody. And I figured that if Jesus could die so that all of my wrongs could be forgiven, I can certainly extend that same grace to you."[11]

What a testimony of grace shared on a nationally televised program! So many times we think we deserve an apology from people who hurt us, and sometimes we are not willing to forgive unless we get one. But Jesus willingly gave His life on the Cross— all the while knowing that many of the people for whom He died would never apologize for their sins or accept His free gift of salvation. But He did it for them anyway.

If Jesus could give His own life to forgive us, can we not find it within ourselves to forgive others?

And now let's look at forgiveness from yet another angle. We must remember that as Christians our willingness to forgive reflects not only upon ourselves but also upon our Lord. We are supposed to be *Christlike* (like Jesus). Our actions are supposed to bring honor to God since we are His representatives on earth. Our attributes as Christians are supposed to be a reflection of His. If we don't forgive others, and if we portray selfish and vindictive spirits, we will lose opportunities for our lives to be witnesses of Christ's willingness to forgive, and our attitudes will cause us to fail in glorifying God before others.

---

11 Transcribed from a video recording of the program.

Our actions toward people can speak louder than our words. And it has been said that our lives are the only Bible some people will read. So let's consider how the way we offer forgiveness can point people to Jesus.

Think of this: It's common for people to expect a negative reaction from people they hurt or offend. There are a good many people (especially unbelievers) who hurt us and actually expect us to retaliate in predictable ways. So why don't we extend grace to them instead of retribution and really throw them for a loop?[12]

Give them forgiveness and point them to Jesus. Our action of being quick to forgive can be the unexpected reaction that is needed to jar them into thinking about their own need for forgiveness by God. The grace you extend to the people who have hurt you might just become the open door through which Jesus allows you to share His love with them.

But what about the times when the person who hurts us is a brother or sister in Christ? Ouch! Unfortunately, many people have told me that their most painful wounds came from the actions of other Christians. Clearly that's not what God wants in the Church.

There is too much that could be said about that to adequately expand on the topic here, but I will say that I understand their pain

---

12 "Do not take revenge, my dear friends, but leave room for God's wrath, for it is written: 'It is mine to avenge; I will repay,' says the Lord. On the contrary: 'If your enemy is hungry, feed him; if he is thirsty, give him something to drink. In doing this, you will heap burning coals on his head.' Do not be overcome by evil, but overcome evil with good" (Romans 12:19-21).

and frustration. As I look back over my own life, I can definitely say that some of my own deepest hurts also were caused by other Christians—people I trusted the most.

We tend to hold our Christian brothers and sisters to a high standard. Rightly or wrongly, we expect more from them than unbelievers. And it can be extremely painful and confusing when they hurt us.

When dealing with our expectations about how fellow Christians should treat us, we must remember that although we are believers, we are all still human. And as such we are still dealing with temptations and weaknesses of the flesh. Fortunately, though, we have God's help to overcome those things.

It will help us to forgive if we stay humble before God. There are times when people just mess up. They make mistakes.[13] Remember in humility that forgiveness dwells where Christ lives. To forgive is a choice, and to offer forgiveness to others when we feel wronged is something that only we can choose to do individually.

Truthfully, even with the enemy of our soul doing everything he can to sow discord in the Church, stir up conflict in our families, and wreak havoc in all our godly relationships, I think Christians do pretty well compared to those outside the Church. But we could do better. We all need to grow, and as we forgive others we continue to make progress in our discipleship as we reveal that we are truly striving to follow Christ.

---

13 "We all stumble in many ways. Anyone who is never at fault in what they say is perfect, able to keep their whole body in check" (James 3:2).

Forgive all who offend you, and forgive your brothers and sisters quickly!

If hurts and offenses are left to fester, they can cause people to break fellowship with others who love them. And in the worst case, unforgiveness can cause people to walk away from both church and God altogether. We must be quick to forgive and not allow our responses to pain encourage such actions in any way.

Always remember how often you yourself have been forgiven. When others hurt you, pray for them even if it's the last thing you want to do. This is how we overcome the pain. Strive to love like Jesus. It may not be easy in every case, but sincere people who are strong in the faith forgive others. Faithless, insincere people who are weak in their commitment to follow Christ's example cling to wrongs and refuse to forgive. Don't be one of them.

There is freedom in forgiveness. Forgive, and you will not only be forgiven, you will grow. God can use us in powerful, amazing ways if we give all our hurts and feelings of injustice over to Him and choose to forgive.

CHAPTER 8

THE TEST OF OBEDIENCE

WHEN I FIRST got an idea of what I thought God was calling me to do (that is, after I accepted it), the very first thing that entered my mind was, "I need to learn more!" I took that thought seriously and began taking action to increase my knowledge in order to be better equipped for ministry. In doing so, I of course studied my Bible as much as possible, but I also felt I needed training and knowledge that I would likely gain only by being involved in a more structured experience. I felt I needed to go back to school, and that is exactly what I did.

I started taking classes through the *Iowa School of Ministry*—an institute-level school dedicated to ministry training through a combination of self-study and live instruction. It was perfect for me as a mom. I had a month to complete the course materials at home. I then attended classes one weekend a month, and that was followed by a final test. I thought I would be thoroughly equipped once I completed the program.

Little did I know, though, that God had also just enrolled me into His own spiritual boot camp, and things were about to get interesting.

I always thought I was fairly obedient when it came to doing what God asked of me—I tried to be, anyway. Still, God was ready to show me what I needed to work on, how I needed to respond to Him and various situations, and how I needed to be *quick* about it. In the Lord's boot camp, one of the first things I learned was that He wanted me to *move* when He said *move*.

The first lesson that came from the Lord's way of training me came late one evening in a grocery store. I was tired, and I really wanted to get home. It was cold and starting to snow, and I didn't want to be caught in a snowstorm.

For some reason my attention was drawn to the young mother in the check-out line in front of me. She had a young baby in an infant seat in her shopping cart. She had probably less than ten items there on the counter to purchase, and I felt the Holy Spirit nudge me and tell me to pay for the things she was purchasing.

It was a simple request, and I had no problem doing it. But I wasn't sure how to go about it, so I stood there thinking about how to approach the situation. Then the thought occurred to me, "What if she takes offense to me paying for her stuff? What if it embarrasses her or makes her feel uncomfortable? She doesn't look like she needs money. She is nicely dressed, and the baby is, too."

All the reasons I shouldn't pay for her things popped into my head. I spent too much time thinking, and she paid for her items while I was still deciding what to do. I began to feel terrible as she pushed away her cart.

The cost of her items totaled less than twenty dollars, but the cost of her purchase really had nothing to do with the reason for our encounter. And whether or not she needed the money was not supposed to be a determining factor in whether or not I should do what I was prompted to do. The fact is, God asked me to do something, and I didn't do it.

I reached into my wallet, pulled out a twenty-dollar bill, and watched her to see where she went. I quickly paid for my purchases and went to find her so I could give her the twenty dollars. I had only turned my head for a moment, but by then she was gone.

"How hard could it be to find her with a baby in tow?" I thought. But then it was as if God whispered, "It's too late."

I knew it was too late for me to be obedient. I knew I had failed a test. I ran into the parking lot and looked everywhere for her, but I never saw her again. I felt horrible all the way home. "Why wasn't I obedient? I thought. "Why did I resist that gentle prompting of the Holy Spirit?"

As I drove down the dark highway toward home, I prayed and said, "God, I am so sorry! I promise I will not let you down next time. Please give me another chance."

Well, the Lord certainly answers prayers! I was in yet another line at the local discount store the very next day, and the lady in front of me didn't have enough money to pay for her things. I quickly stepped up and said, "Let me pay for this."

Both the cashier and the lady in need looked at me, but neither of them said a word. I paid for her purchases, and she left without so much as a "Thank you." Then the cashier looked at me and said, "Why did you do that?"

I told him, "God has blessed me, and if I have the opportunity to bless others I feel like I should do that."

He simply responded with, "I've just never seen anyone do that before."

Maybe the Lord knew the cashier needed to see the blessing the customer received more than the customer actually needed the blessing. Either way, though, I had been obedient. And I thought that maybe I had made up for the previous failure to respond to the Holy Spirit's prompting. But the story about that particular lesson the Lord was teaching me doesn't end there.

A few days later I was in Walmart, and there was a lady in front of me at checkout. She swiped her credit card to pay for her items, and it didn't work. She swiped it again to no avail. The checkout clerk said, "Do you have another form of payment?" Immediately, I swiped my card and paid for her things.

The woman looked at me with a bewildered expression, and then said, "You didn't have to do that." I told her that I wanted to, and told her to have a blessed day.

Twice in a row? At this point I was saying, "OK God, I get it now."

The following week, in yet another store, I was once again in line at another check-out counter, when, guess what? The man in line in front of me didn't have enough money to pay.

Let me just insert this here: I did not live in a poverty-stricken area. These experiences were far from normal. Clearly God was teaching me a lesson, and I understand now how valuable that lesson was.

I guess the Lord realized that for me to learn the entire lesson it would take three times for me to experience it—like the number of times it took for a certain experience to sink in for Peter.[14] But regardless, I learned the lesson. I quickly stepped up and paid for the man's items. He thanked me and went on his way.

That was it. Three times in a row, and then everyone around me seemed to have plenty of money. This may sound

---

14 "Peter replied, 'Even if all fall away on account of you, I never will.'

'Truly I tell you,' Jesus answered, 'this very night, before the rooster crows, you will disown me three times.'

. . . Now Peter was sitting out in the courtyard, and a servant girl came to him. 'You also were with Jesus of Galilee,' she said. But he denied it before them all. 'I don't know what you're talking about,' he said. Then he went out to the gateway, where another girl saw him and said to the people there, 'This fellow was with Jesus of Nazareth.' He denied it again, with an oath: 'I don't know the man!' After a little while, those standing there went up to Peter and said, 'Surely you are one of them; your accent gives you away.' Then he began to call down curses, and he swore to them, 'I don't know the man!'

Immediately a rooster crowed. Then Peter remembered the word Jesus had spoken: 'Before the rooster crows, you will disown me three times.' And he went outside and wept bitterly" (Matthew 26:33-34 & 69-75).

far-fetched, but I promise you that is exactly how it happened. So now as I go about living life I watch for opportunities to help, and I listen intently for God's instructions. Listening to God is important for all Christians regardless of how the Lord may want to use us in ministry.

For me, Lesson One in God's spiritual boot camp was complete.

My next lesson in obedience came completely out of the blue. I was taking part in an online Christian forum where many people posted prayer requests. There was a lady on the website talking about how she had been struggling with depression since her divorce, and she said she really needed prayer.

I quickly replied to her post and said, "I'm so sorry to hear that you are going through this. I've been there. If I can pray with you, or if you would just like to talk to someone, e-mail me."

And with that I left my e-mail address for her. As soon as I hit the send button, I noticed it had disappeared. I thought that was strange, but since I was in a hurry I decided to leave it alone.

The next day I received a message from someone I did not know. She explained that she was from the Christian forum and had somehow received my message. She said, "I don't even know why I'm e-mailing you. I was just shocked to see what you said to me. I didn't even say in my post that anything was wrong!"

I went back to the website and found that my comment had somehow landed on the post of someone else—not the one for whom it was intended.

She e-mailed me again, and in the next e-mail she began to pour out her heart to me. She told me she had been struggling a long time, and my comment was an answer to her prayer. She also told me she had done so much wrong in her life that God could never forgive her.

I then began to explain to her how God loved her, and He would forgive her for anything.

She said, "You just don't know how terrible I am!"

I told her, "Everyone makes mistakes, but we are still loved by God; and all we need to do is ask Him to forgive us, believe in Jesus, and accept Him as our Savior."

But she still disagreed with me, and the next e-mail she sent to me was more than shocking. She told me everything. She said she was a prostitute, and that she was also involved in the porn industry as an actress. Then she said she had become pregnant by one of her clients, had an abortion, and now spent most of her days drunk—trying to cope with what she was doing with her life. My head was spinning.

I raised my face toward heaven and said, "God, what on earth are you thinking? I'm not prepared for this! I can't counsel this lady and provide the help she needs. I'm far too inadequate for this."

Yet, the Lord sent her to me, so I wrote back to her. I told her that God would forgive her for all her past deeds, and I told her that He still loved her no matter what she had done. I then gave her my telephone number and asked her to call me.

She wrote back and told me she didn't want to talk to me because she was ashamed for me to even hear her voice after telling me all that she revealed to me. But she did start texting me.

We spent several days texting back and forth, and I tried my best to pour the love of God into her. I told her that I loved her, too. It was clear that she began to trust me, so I finally asked her if I could just call her and talk; and I told her she wouldn't have to say anything if she didn't want to.

She agreed, so I called and shared my testimony with her. I told her of the immense love that God has for His children, including her, and that His love is not like the love of this world. I could hear her weeping on the other end of the phone. I then asked her if she would like to pray.

She yelled back, "I can't do this!"

The phone call ended abruptly; she was gone, and I felt horrible. I thought maybe I pushed her too hard, too soon. In the next moment, though, that still small voice of the Holy Spirit whispered to me, "Text her and tell her that what happened to her as a little girl was not her fault."

I said, "God, I can't do that. I have no idea if anything happened to her as a little girl!"

But the urgency that I felt to text her seemed to grow stronger. Then before I could argue for another second, I remembered the young lady in the grocery store and my missed opportunity. So I entered those words into my phone, and before pressing *Send*

I prayed one last time that if the Lord didn't really mean that message for her it would somehow get lost in cyberspace.

I'm not kidding!

It was actually less than a minute after I sent the text that my phone started ringing. She was on the other end, and she was absolutely sobbing. She said, "How did you know that? I have never told anyone about that. How could you possibly know?"

I told her, "I didn't know anything, but God loves you so much He wanted you to know that it was not your fault."

We cried together for a while, and then she said, "I'm ready now. I want to ask Jesus to come into my heart." We prayed together, and she accepted Christ as her Savior that very day.

And that was my completion of Lesson Two in boot camp—with Lesson Three soon to come.

I was visiting my mom in Tennessee a couple of months later. I was crocheting a scarf for her, and I had just run out of yarn. I stopped by Walmart to pick up more yarn, and as I was looking for the color I needed I noticed two ladies on the same aisle looking at yarn.

There was nothing special about the ladies that would have caught my attention, but suddenly I had the feeling I had swallowed about a hundred butterflies, and they were all doing somersaults in my stomach.

That's when I heard the Holy Spirit whisper to me, "I want you to pray for those ladies." I thought, "Oh no! Not here, God. Not now."

I kept trying to talk the Lord out of making me do it, but I eventually came to feel like I absolutely had to. I thought I might actually lose my lunch right there in the store if I didn't obey—those butterflies were wreaking havoc in my tummy.

I argued with God, "But they are going to think I'm crazy. I can't just walk up and start praying for them!"

But the Lord didn't relent, so I slowly walked up to them. It appeared they were a mom and daughter. The daughter looked like she was probably in her mid-twenties. I softly said, "I know you two are probably going to think I'm crazy, but God just told me to come over here and ask if I could pray with you about something. Is there anything I can pray with you about?"

I could feel my face beginning to flush as they looked at me, but when I looked at the young lady, I saw that she now had tears in her eyes.

The young lady's mom said, "My daughter could certainly use some prayer."

I then asked the daughter if it was OK for me to pray with her right there in the middle of the store, and she said, "Yes."

I gently placed my hand on her arm, and immediately the Holy Spirit took over. I can't even remember everything I said to her, or prayed for her, but she began openly crying. Tears were flowing from her eyes as well as her mom's eyes.

I was amazed by the powerful presence of the Holy Spirit surrounding us in that precious moment. After I finished praying, I told her, "God must certainly have big plans for you, because the Lord sent me to pray with you in a store while I was visiting in Tennessee. I actually live in Iowa."

She looked astonished. I hugged her and turned to leave, and as I left I could hear her mother say to her, "I told you so, I told you so, I told you so!" They were then laughing and crying tears of joy.

I wish I could have known the whole situation, but it wasn't for me to know. They knew the situation, and God knew their need. As I've said many times, our God is a good Father. He longs to encourage His children and meet their needs. And He wants us to be available—listening for His voice—so we can be His hands and feet as He reaches out to people in need.

When it came to my participation in the Lord's actions of reaching out to people in need—as illustrated in my lessons learned in God's spiritual boot camp—it was clear to me that none of the good that came out of those experiences depended on my own knowledge, wisdom, and understanding. God is the one who understood each situation and actually held the solutions for those in need. But when it came to those people actually receiving what God had for them, what if I hadn't been obedient?

I believe that was the point of those lessons.

It is only through God's power to meet needs that spiritual problems are solved, lives are salvaged, and the redeemed are set free. But God chooses to use us to deliver His solutions to those in need. He called us—the Church—to do that.

Who will be the voice of God to those who desperately need Him if we are not obedient?

The Lord is still teaching me, and I'm confident that I will never stop learning from Him. There are many more stories I could tell you about the way the Holy Spirit has tutored and discipled me in both life and ministry. The lessons and the tests that He has administered to me during my spiritual training have sometimes been difficult for me. Some lessons have been easier, and some lessons have been harder, but they have all been what I needed.

Every lesson in life is associated with a test. And I have found that every test I have passed has led to a promotion of some kind. Being taught, taking tests, taking the lessons over, and taking tests until we pass—this is how we grow.

God knows what He is doing in our discipleship. And the Holy Spirit is a wonderful tutor. He starts by teaching us simple things, but He doesn't stop there. He goes on to teach us progressively more challenging lessons.

The lessons may get harder as we grow in faith, but with the passing of each test, our tendency to hear and be obedient to the Lord's leading also grows. And as we grow in obedience and faith, God entrusts us with more and more responsibility to do His will in a world that needs Him so desperately.

CHAPTER 9

INTIMACY WITH GOD

SEVERAL YEARS AGO, I was a member of the prayer team in my home church. One Sunday morning at church, when our pastor gave the altar call, a few people went forward for salvation. I felt led to pray for a middle-aged lady kneeling at the altar less than 10 feet away from me.

As I began to talk to her about her relationship with Christ, she informed me she didn't have one, and she said she had never asked Jesus to come into her heart. After talking with her about Jesus and His plan for our salvation, I led her in prayer, and she accepted Christ as her Savior.

As we continued to talk, I will never forget what she asked me. She looked me right in the eye and said, "How do I *love* Jesus?"

It was an honest question straight from her heart. She began to explain to me that she had never had a male influence in her life—at least one that had been anything but abusive and hurtful. She honestly wanted to know how to love this *man*, Jesus.

I was stopped dead in my tracks. It was a simple question, but I had no words.

What could I say? I had grown up in church, and I had been taught about Jesus in Sunday school all through my youth. Even after making the mistake of walking away from Him, I also had the joy of coming home to Him and experiencing His mercy, forgiveness, and grace. I *knew* Him, and I found Him easy to love because of what I knew.

Yet there before me was a woman who as a child had not had the luxury of sitting in front of a flannelboard and seeing all the colorful pictures of Jesus, His disciples, and His miracles. She had not had the joy of sitting in a peaceful Sunday school classroom, singing songs about Jesus, and coloring picture pages with Scripture verses on them.

No, here was a woman who had been abused as a young girl by her father and beaten repeatedly by one man after another through multiple relationships. And she had just left her husband— who almost killed her. In her mind, she was being encouraged to ask a *man* to forgive *her* of her sins and come into her life, when in her experience there were so many men who needed to seek forgiveness from her.

My heart flooded with compassion as I realized how hard it must be for her to trust again. Even though she clearly felt the drawing of the Holy Spirit and love of our heavenly Father, how *could* she trust again?

In the next moment God gave me a simple illustration that helped me answer her question. In my mind I saw a woman standing at a bus stop. A complete stranger walked up to her and asked her to marry him. She said, "Yes!" Then they walked away together in perfect happiness.

I thought to myself, "God, that would never happen. There is no way a woman would marry a man she had never seen or talked to before in her life!"

That's when it hit me: It's not easy to immediately love someone you don't know.

I told her, "You have to get to know Jesus. You have to read the Bible and learn about His character. You have to see that He is trustworthy and faithful, and that He loves you with an unconditional love! You have to get to *know* Him!"

I shared with her all the things the Lord had done for me, how He had never left me, and how He had never given up on me. I encouraged her to talk to Jesus like a friend. And although I could not control her response to my encouragement, it turned out that after leaving the church that day she went home and actually began following my advice.

She began spending time reading the Bible. She also became a regular attender in our services and allowed herself regular, weekly opportunities to be discipled by the pastoral staff and others in the church. As I observed over time, she began to grow in the Lord. She continued to read the Word of God and spend time in prayer, and I saw her countenance seemingly brighten from Sunday to Sunday.

I think sometimes we get frustrated with baby Christians because we don't see immediate changes in their lives—at least the changes we expect to see. We need to practice patience. And after the experience I had with the dear Sister I just described, I now wonder if the slow progress in spiritual growth that I sometimes observe in some believers is simply an indication that they just haven't made the effort to really get to know Jesus.

We must encourage newly-birthed Christians to get to *know* Jesus. Knowing Jesus is knowing God,[15] and there is nothing more important, or more exciting, than developing an intimate relationship with our heavenly Father.

I understand now that for many years I tried to make my own relationship with Christ work by just going through the motions without really knowing Jesus. I thought if I went to church and didn't drink, smoke, swear, lie, cheat, or steal, I was doing all I needed to do to be a *good* Christian.

After all, I was following all *the rules.*

There are many people who think they are good Christians, but who never pick up the Bible to read about Christ and God's expectations for them. There are many who never say a prayer outside of asking the blessing over their food before eating. Many

---

15 "Jesus answered, 'I am the way and the truth and the life. No one comes to the Father except through me. If you really know me, you will know my Father as well. From now on, you do know him and have seen him'" (John 14:6-7).

people appear to do all the things Christians do, and they even follow *the rules*, but they seemingly don't know Jesus at all. There is nothing more important than a personal relationship with Christ. That's the only way we are truly going to come to know God.

Again, knowing Jesus is knowing God, so no one will actually come to *know* God without doing what's necessary to establish a personal relationship with Jesus. And without doubt, no one will do what is necessary to establish and maintain a relationship with Jesus without being committed to the task—without making it a priority.

Knowing the importance of developing a personal relationship with our Lord, I never pray for people to receive salvation anymore without asking them if they realize they are entering into a relationship that requires commitment. Just like in a successful marriage, we must put forth an effort to do more than just follow a few simple rules. For a marriage to work, one's relationship with his or her spouse must go far beyond keeping or not breaking rules. And so it is with our relationship with God.

Jesus loves us, but do we love Him back? Do we honor Him? The Lord certainly knows us—inside and out—but do we really know who *He* is? If we don't get to know Him, how will we establish with Him a true and lasting relationship filled with and motivated by love?

My sheep listen to my voice; I know them, and they follow me.

(John 10:27)

Sheep come to know their shepherd, and they learn to not only recognize his voice but also follow him when he calls to them. Do we spend enough time with God to get to know Him that way? Do we get to know Him to the point of being willing to entrust our future and safety to Him as He leads us? Do we recognize His voice? How can we follow Him and remain secure in our relationship if we don't know His voice?

I love my daughters dearly. When they were very small, I could recognize their cries in the middle of a room full of other crying babies. In the same way, they could recognize my voice when they were upset and would hush their crying to hear my voice more clearly. Even now I recognize their voices first in a group of people. They are my children, and I am their mother. I know them, and they know me.

In a world full of voices vying for our attention—many of which are destructive rather than helpful—there is one voice that should always be louder and clearer than any other to us. The voice of Jesus should always be the one we are listening for above all others; after all, we are His, and He is ours. But if we are not willing to spend time with Him, we are not likely to learn His voice.

I remember shopping with my mom when I was about five years old. I would often get bored as we wandered up and down aisles and in between racks of clothing in different stores. On one occasion, I was straggling behind my mom, and my mind was apparently off in my own little world. Not paying attention, I reached out and grabbed the hand of a lady standing near me, assuming she was my mom.

She smiled at me and said, "Honey, I think you are probably looking for your mother."

I was frightened the instant I heard her voice. I then looked up at her unfamiliar face and immediately jerked my hand away! That clearly was NOT the sound of my mother's voice. Quickly looking around, I noticed my mom was only a few steps ahead of me, and I ran to her. Only a few seconds of taking my eyes off my mom caused me to mistakenly grab hold of a stranger's hand.

Just as a child can become distracted and get separated from a parent in a store, if we don't stick close to Jesus we can also allow ourselves to become distracted in our Christian walk.

And think of this: Unlike the woman whose voice actually directed me toward my mother—the woman whose hand I reached out and took in my distraction—always remember that Satan wants nothing more than to purposely come up beside us and offer us his hand in an attempt to lead us astray. And he will not try to straighten up confusion. He will attempt to mimic our Father's voice. Beware, because to the unsuspecting person who has become sidetracked he can appear to be something he's not, and his deception can be convincing.[16]

---

16 "For such people are false apostles, deceitful workers, masquerading as apostles of Christ. And no wonder, for Satan himself masquerades as an angel of light. It is not surprising, then, if his servants also masquerade as servants of righteousness. Their end will be what their actions deserve" (2 Corinthians 11:13-15).

Children of God who have a close, intimate relationship with their heavenly Father will not be fooled. They will stay focused. But even if in a moment of weakness they are distracted, they will quickly recognize if they have grabbed the wrong hand. Just like I knew my mother, they know the Lord, and they will jerk away and run to their Father in a challenging situation.

We must gain knowledge and have a sincere relationship with Christ if we are to be successful in living a life that is pleasing to Him—a life that is in line with what the Bible reveals is expected of His followers. As members of His flock, we must follow our Shepherd as He directs us. Keeping our eyes on the Shepherd, listening to His voice, and trusting God, we follow Him. And following only Him keeps us from going astray as He guides us in the path that leads toward green pastures, where we find our sustenance.[17]

As I have followed Jesus, I have come to agree with David that we really are sustained by God, our Shepherd. By following Christ we find what we truly need. But I have discovered that the Great Shepherd is not only interested in sustaining us, He is also interested in guiding us into ministry and enabling us to lead others to Him so they can have their needs met, too. So He is leading me not only for my own, personal benefit but also for the benefit of others.

It should be natural and completely normal for all Christians to want to possess something of value to provide to others. And when I minister, I believe it is precisely my own intimate

---

17 Psalms 23.

relationship with Christ, my Shepherd, that causes me to feel obligated to have something fresh from the heart of God to give to listeners each time I have an opportunity to speak for Him. So I seek God for that.

When we draw close and stay close to Him, He can lead us in how we minister to others and in what we say. As we follow our Shepherd, He will not only provide to us what we need, personally, and lead us into ministry, He will provide things of value for us to share with those to whom we minister. He will lead us in every way.

The Holy Spirit pours out His anointing on believers who have come to know and obey His voice. He empowers them so their lives might also affect others to know Jesus and come into relationship with Him. When we show the Lord that we are willing to seek His heart and speak His message to others, He can and will minister through us. And I feel extremely humbled and blessed when that happens in my life.

It's a wonderful thing to be used of God. When I have the privilege to minister God's Word and will to others, I feel there is a very special, spiritual communion taking place between our Shepherd and me. There is something so sweet and so intimate about knowing and having confidence that He is in control. There is nothing in the world so fulfilling to me than knowing God is using me for His glory at that very moment.

When I step off the platform after ministering for the Lord in a church, when I see people on their knees before God, seeking His face, and giving their lives to Him, there is such a joy that floods my soul! And when I am able to see what the Lord is doing in the lives of those to whom I have ministered, in that moment I feel as if God approvingly smiles down on me.

But I have an acute understanding that I gain His approval not because I have simply shared His Word with others—performed a good work—but because I am merely exhibiting that I have an intimate relationship with Him. Because of the intimacy I have with God, He is keeping me going in the right direction—the path He has prepared for my life and ministry.

There is nothing in this whole world that excites me more than feeling like I have pleased my heavenly Father. And even though I believe I already have a spiritually enriching, intimate relationship with Him now, I still long to be closer to Jesus. All of us should continue to strive to more thoroughly know Him and His voice. We all need to become ever-closer to God and more knowledgeable about His ways. There is nothing better than knowing the Lord, loving Him, and serving Him every day.

CHAPTER 10

WAITING

WHEN I GAVE birth to my first child, in addition to having my husband, Bryan, there with me for the delivery, I also wanted my mom in the delivery room. And she wanted to be there just as much as I wanted her there. That was one of the most exciting events of my life, and Mom had always been a witness to so many of my life's big events.

The doctor decided to induce my labor because of some health concerns, and I was already in labor when my mom and dad arrived at the hospital. I was looking forward to seeing them, but I did not get to talk to them when they arrived. You see, the anesthesiologist had administered a spinal epidural anesthesia to me just minutes before. The pain I was experiencing then subsided, and I fell asleep from total exhaustion—and probably with a little help from the IV meds.

When my parents came into the room they saw me sound asleep, totally oblivious to the world. They obviously thought it was going to be a long while before their first granddaughter was born. So they decided to go back out to the lobby and wait.

Evidently the minute they walked out of the room, though, I woke up to the nurse telling me it was time to push.

The next thing I knew, the doctor blazed into the room and stood at the foot of my bed. After a few intense pushes, he held up before me a tiny, pink, baby girl! Bryan cut the umbilical cord and went to the lobby to get my parents. He walked in and asked them if they wanted to see their grandbaby. They thought he was kidding.

Mom and Dad had literally just entered the waiting area. If they had only waited five more minutes! My mom couldn't believe she missed the birth since I was sleeping so soundly when they left the room.

Two years later, when I was delivering my second child, my mom was sure she was not going to miss that delivery. I was admitted into the hospital around 9:00 PM, and even after the doctor started inducing my labor it seemed like nothing was happening. I slept peacefully through the night, and my parents arrived early the next morning.

I tossed and turned in that uncomfortable hospital bed all day until late that afternoon when the labor pains finally kicked in. Then, like before, the anesthesiologist came in and administered the epidural. And before long I was once again feeling fine.

And similar to what happened when our first child was born, seeing that I was no longer in pain, my parents again assumed the baby wouldn't be there for several more hours. They had been at the hospital all day, and they were exhausted; so they decided to go back home. I found out later that Mom and Dad actually crossed paths with my doctor in the hallway on their way out. And guess what? She was on her way to my room.

My doctor came into my room, examined me, and told me to start pushing. I could not believe it was happening again! After only a few pushes, there was my second little baby girl. Bryan again left right after he cut the umbilical cord, and he ran to the parking lot. He was sure that he could catch my parents before they left. But it was too late!

Bryan watched as Mom and Dad were just pulling out of the parking lot onto the highway. This was before my parents had become mobile phone users, so we couldn't call them until they arrived home—and home was 45 minutes away. Once again, if they had only waited five more minutes!

When I think back on those two instances, I can't help but wonder just how many times I have also missed something wonderful because I didn't wait long enough. Perhaps God had something great in store for me, but I didn't wait long enough to receive it. Perhaps I was expecting something from God but gave up and missed it even though I had been praying about it for months. Maybe I was just about to receive a miracle but didn't receive it because of my impatience. Maybe from my perspective it appeared nothing was happening, so I went my way and missed God's plan.

I once heard someone say, "God answers prayers in three ways: 'Yes,' 'Not now,' or, 'I have something better!'" When we don't receive something from the Lord in the time we expect, how many times do we interpret His delay as a definite "NO" and just give up? Knowing my own lack of patience, I would be afraid to find out about all the opportunities that have passed me by because I gave up just a moment too soon—because I didn't wait.

Sometimes it's so hard to be patient and wait, and I believe we often struggle with patience because we have trouble seeing things from God's perspective. We may only see what seems to be happening from our narrow views of situations as they appear on the surface. But God sees every small detail. He knows exactly what He is working on and how He's putting it all together.

Maybe the Lord is answering us, "Yes, but not right now," but we aren't hearing it. And maybe we aren't hearing it because we don't expect or even want to hear that answer.

God's timing is perfect. He always knows how long it takes to fulfill His plans. But I have found that I am often too impatient to wait for *perfect* timing. I know there have been times when I have interpreted what I perceived as His delay in answering my prayers as a definite "No," when, if I were really listening, I could have heard Him say, "Hold on, I have something else in store for you!"

While I admit I still struggle with impatience, the Lord taught me a lesson once that really cemented into my mind the way God patiently and faithfully works in our lives and ministries—and how there is real benefit in waiting before him until He can fulfill His plans for us. Through this experience I learned the true value of waiting and gained an increased appreciation for the Holy Spirit's leading:

When I first began speaking for churches other than where I was a member, a pastor contacted me from Wisconsin. He asked me to come there and conduct a women's conference for the ladies in the church. It was a small church within easy driving distance of my home in Iowa, and I was so excited I could hardly wait! He told me they were thinking of having the conference around the eleventh of September, but he said he would let me know for sure in a few days.

Then I didn't hear anything else from him. I waited patiently for a couple of weeks, when I finally sent an e-mail to him. In the e-mail I asked him if everything was still set for September.

He said, "Well, I'm not sure, but I think so. Our women's director is having some problems, but I will get back to you in a few days."

I started praying, "God, please let this work out; I desperately want to speak for this women's conference!"

Days passed, and I didn't hear from the pastor. Then came the day I felt as if God was saying, "No, I'm not going to let you speak for this conference!"

I was so discouraged. It was a good opportunity for me to give up on having a speaking engagement that weekend. It was a good time for me to stop waiting and move on!

Then a day later, Rachel Allen, a women's director in Miami Lakes, Florida contacted me and asked me to be a keynote speaker for her *Girl on Fire* women's conference. I was shocked!

Unfortunately it was the same weekend that I had scheduled with the church in Wisconsin.

I told her I was booked for that weekend, and said, "I'm so sorry; I would love to be able to speak at the conference."

She then responded, "Maybe I'm wrong in doing this, but I'm going to pray that Wisconsin reschedules their conference."

We laughed about it at the time, but she and I both felt I needed to be at her conference in Florida.

Soon after that, I decided to contact the pastor in Wisconsin one more time to see if the conference they were planning was still going to happen. I felt like I needed to tell him that I had been asked to speak in Florida that same weekend and ask him to please let me know if their conference was not going to materialize. To my surprise, the pastor told me he was resigning from the church, and he told me I should go ahead and take the invitation from Florida.

I immediately contacted Rachel in Florida to ask if she still needed a speaker. She said, "Yes!" And before I knew it, they booked my flight, made my hotel reservation, and everything was set to go. I couldn't believe it was happening. Someone actually thought I was *worth* the cost of a plane ticket and hotel expense? This was the first time I flew on a plane to speak somewhere, and I honestly couldn't believe it was really happening.

"Why would they even want me?" I thought. As far as I knew, nobody had even heard of me at that point in my ministry. But there I was in Miami, Florida.

During the time I was waiting for the church in Wisconsin to confirm my speaking engagement there, I was terrified that the Wisconsin church would change its mind and decide against having me come. I was so afraid that God was going to answer my request for the Lord to allow me to speak there with a giant, "NO!" Yet all the while He was simply saying, "Hold on daughter, I've got something else for you to do."

There I was in Florida, and I could not believe how pampered I was while I was at the conference in Miami. It was one of the best *first* experiences ever! I spoke for the opening session on Saturday morning, and I also spoke in two workshops that day. I was in awe of the things God accomplished there in the hearts and lives of the ladies in attendance. Many ladies came to me and told me how blessed they were by my testimony. That whole experience was a huge encouragement to me.

There is no doubt in my mind that I was meant to be there. It became absolutely crystal clear to me. God knew exactly what He was doing. While I was begging God for something that He knew was not going to happen, He was preparing another avenue of ministry for me. While I was on the verge of giving up on having an opportunity for ministry that weekend, the Lord had it all under control. I just needed to be patient and wait.

I needed to give him just *five more minutes*!

I feel like my Heavenly Father allowed me to go through that experience for the express purpose of showing me I can afford to wait on Him to act. I can afford to have patience when

He is leading. He wanted to show me through that experience exactly what He could do if I would only be patient and wait for His answer.

Clearly, waiting is sometimes so hard! But with faith and the Lord's strength, we can do it.

As I was writing the first draft of this chapter in my book, I was actually in a season of waiting on God; and that particular season of waiting proved to be one of the longest, most frustrating periods in my life. But I decided at the time to continue to place my confidence in Christ for the future.

I determined in my mind at that time not to allow myself to be discouraged and forget what I had seen God do so many times before in my life. A season of waiting challenged me, but it didn't last forever. And as each season of waiting ends for me (and we all have them from time to time), I continue to choose to believe that it is well worth waiting for the things the Lord has in store for my future. And you can count on His plans for your future, too.

Here is one of my favorite verses to remind me that God knows what is ahead, and that He has our best interests at heart. It always encourages me, and I hope it encourages you as well.

However, as it is written: "What no eye has seen, what no ear has heard, and what no human mind has conceived"—the things God has prepared for those who love him—these are the things God has revealed to us by his Spirit.

(1 Corinthians 2:9-10a)

God will not always keep us waiting. It is not in His nature to continually withhold His plans from His people. You see, God is in the business of revelation. He is in the business of revealing to us things that remain hidden from those who cannot conceive of the things that only His Spirit reveals. We are so blessed!

We cannot know what God has prepared for us before He acts to reveal it; but we can be assured that He will continue to reveal His plan to us step by step as we continue in our obedience to Him and maintain our faith in His leadership.

By His Spirit He has already revealed to us His wonderful plan for our salvation; He has already revealed to us many things that the mere human mind cannot conceive. And He will not cease to reveal to us His plans for our continuing discipleship and the ministries into which He calls us. Our part is to trust Him and, when necessary, wait patiently for that next revelation.

There is a song that I often put on "repeat" in my CD player. I listen to it over and over. It has encouraged me and helped me through so many seasons of waiting. It is based on the verses in Psalms 130. The name of the song is *Out of the Depths* by Bob Kauflin.

In the song Bob begins by using the words of the psalmist: "Out of the depths I cry to you, O Lord." Then he uses more of the psalmist's words, and the psalm's theme, to express his resolute intention to wait for the Lord because he chooses to place his trust in God.

The words of that song express my heart and confidence in the Lord. I don't like to wait. But when it is necessary, I am determined to do it. I invite you to wait with me. And if you do, I'm sure we will one day rejoice together as we look back over what the Lord was able to do in our lives—lives through which we patiently allowed him to work.

CHAPTER 11

HEARING FROM GOD

HAVE YOU EVER wished you could have a conversation with God that would be just like sharing a telephone call with a friend? I certainly have. I've even hoped for Him to speak to me with a loud, booming voice from Heaven. Especially when I'm asking Him for direction, or how to make a decision, I wish He would just walk in the door and give me the answer.

Unfortunately, it doesn't quite work that way—at least for me. But the good news is, He does speak to us! It's just not always how we wish or expect. To hear from God, we must learn how He speaks to us, and we must come to recognize His voice when He does speak.

So, how do we recognize His voice, and in what ways is He speaking to us? First, there's the most obvious way: He speaks to us through His Word, the Holy Bible.

For the word of God is alive and active. Sharper than any double-edged sword, it penetrates even to dividing soul and

spirit, joints and marrow; it judges the thoughts and attitudes
of the heart.   (Hebrews 4:12)

The Word of God is "alive and active." This is one of my favorite scriptures, because it tells us the wonderful Holy Bible we are reading is not just an old history book full of stories passed down through the ages. No, it is alive and active, and it contains the actual message of the Risen Savior—the Living God!

For us, that means when we seek God's direction about something, we can often get exactly what we need by simply reading the Bible. When I have faced problems or difficult issues, I can't tell you how many times I picked up my Bible, opened it, and soon found comfort and direction from the words I read.

God speaks to us through His Holy Word. There are times when I read something in the Bible, and it seems as if the words just leap off the page at me. I may have read a passage before a hundred times or more, but in those moments, its words just hit me with such full force and revelation that I just know God is speaking to me right then and there.

We know that *"all Scripture is God-breathed"* (2 Timothy 3:16), and it is the Holy Spirit who enlightens us by imparting to us wisdom, knowledge, and understanding so that in times of need, the Word has an immediate impact upon us. It's almost as if the Holy Spirit shines a physical light on the Scriptures—to illuminate them in such a way that we feel as if the Father himself is delivering the very words into our hearts.

Daily Bible reading brings to us great comfort and enlightenment, and it's such a special joy to know that in particular times of despair, stress, or any other challenging situation, we can go to the Bible for answers. We can go to God's Word and hear God's voice speaking to us through His living Word.

———

But getting back to where I started this chapter, wouldn't it be nice if the Lord would just speak aloud to us? On this topic I am once again reminded of one of my favorite passages in First Kings (I quoted this in a footnote in Chapter 1):

The Lord said, "Go out and stand on the mountain in the presence of the Lord, for the Lord is about to pass by."

Then a great and powerful wind tore the mountains apart and shattered the rocks before the Lord, but the Lord was not in the wind. After the wind there was an earthquake, but the Lord was not in the earthquake. After the earthquake came a fire, but the Lord was not in the fire. And after the fire came a gentle whisper. When Elijah heard it, he pulled his cloak over his face and went out and stood at the mouth of the cave.

Then a voice said to him, "What are you doing here, Elijah?"

(1 Kings 19:11-13)

God does still speak to us. But so many times, I think, we are listening for a big booming voice while God is gently whispering to us. We must learn to quiet ourselves, tune out the distractions in our lives, and just listen.

There are people who claim to have heard the audible voice of God. I have not had that experience, but I certainly have had Him speak a word so strongly and so clearly to my heart that it was almost as if I had heard it with my ears. It was as if the weight of the words were so impactful that I literally had to stop and question if I indeed *had* heard an audible voice.

One example of this happening took place shortly after we moved to Iowa from Tennessee. I was missing all my friends and family, and especially my home church. I was walking up the stairs in my home with a laundry basket full of clothes, and in frustration, I just spoke out loud, "God, why in the world did you bring me to Iowa?"

Mine was a desperate cry that came straight from my heart; and the reply I received in return was immediate. It carried with it the sweet tone of empathy and compassion.

The words that echoed throughout my entire being was this simple phrase: "For such a time as this."

I had instant peace and a sense of knowing that everything was going to be alright, because God had brought me to that place "for such a time as this." Just as He positioned Esther in place for a special purpose—to deliver her people (Esther 4:14), God had positioned me there for that particular season, and He had a plan and purpose for doing it.

At that time, I had no idea just what the full context of those words would mean in my life. But that short phrase became the very expression of my entire existence in Iowa. You see, it was in Iowa that God called me to be a women's minister. Those very words were a foreshadowing of what God would do in and through me—and how He would begin to use me in His Kingdom Work.

Another example of when I knew God was speaking to me was during a time of stress and worry about my mother's well-being. She had been having some health problems, and she was seeing her doctor in Tennessee, while I was living in Iowa. Her appointment had been early in the morning, and a short while after lunch, I had still heard nothing from either her or my dad.

I was pursuing my ministerial studies and sitting at the kitchen table doing my homework assignment, when I stopped and just asked God to please be with my mom and comfort both of us. As quickly as I uttered the words, an ominous reply hit my heart and spirit like a tidal wave. These words pierced me to the bone: "Your mom has cancer, but she is going to be OK."

Those words were such a shock to my system, but at the same time, they were accompanied by a peaceful feeling of assurance.

It was literally only a matter of minutes after those words had time to sink in that the phone rang, and I heard my brother crying on the other end of the phone call as he told me that mom had colon cancer. The announcement was of course one of the most horrific things a person can hear, so I collapsed into a crying, frantic mess. But the echo of God's words, "She is going to be OK," hung in the air as if God had just been sitting at the table reassuring me.

It was those words that carried me through the whole process of mom's cancer treatments and the successful surgical removal of her cancer. What I heard from God was absolutely right; my mom had cancer, and the prognosis was not good. But after all the treatments, she was OK.

The Lord showed His faithfulness over and over during her treatment and recovery. When we were told that the cancer was 6 inches long, and a colostomy was inevitable, we began to pray. We asked God to make a way to repair her colon without a colostomy. The Lord's words swept over me again, "She is going to be OK." He answered our prayers, and she did not need a colostomy.

When we were told mom would need to undergo an intense form of radiation intravenously, we began to pray again. God intervened again, and she was able to take a less invasive type of radiation in pill form. One after another, we brought every frightening situation concerning her cancer to the Lord in prayer, and in each and every case, He answered.

God's words to me were a great comfort because I couldn't always be with my mom since we lived so far apart. I held onto those words with all my heart, "She is going to be OK." As of this writing, mom has now been cancer-free for three years.

There are also times when God chooses to speak to us through another person.

Now to each one the manifestation of the Spirit is given for the common good. To one there is given through the Spirit a message of wisdom, to another a message of knowledge by means of the same Spirit, to another faith by the same Spirit, to another gifts of healing by that one Spirit, to another miraculous powers, to another prophecy, to another distinguishing between spirits, to another speaking in different kinds of tongues, and to still another the interpretation of tongues. All these are the work of one and the same Spirit, and he distributes them to each one, just as he determines. (1 Corinthians 12:7-11)

First Corinthians chapter twelve, verses eight through ten, tells us about the gifts of the Holy Spirit. Of the nine gifts listed in this passage, five of them are related to ways that God speaks to us.

Sometimes a message in tongues will be given by a believer during a church service as one of these five gifts is demonstrated, and it is then followed by an interpretation. This is one example of how God speaks to the church through individual believers in order to build up, or edify and encourage the congregation.

Some may have the gift of prophecy and may be able to speak to the church or into people's lives about the future God has for them.

As you may recall what I wrote in a previous chapter, God used another women's minister to speak into my life and give me a tiny glimpse of the future God was leading me into. I don't know if I would have ever believed that I was capable of doing what I do now without that message spoken to me through a complete stranger. Those words were a confirmation to me about the desires God had already fused into my spirit, and they gave me the faith to step out and pursue the calling He had placed on my life.

Some may have the gift of knowledge, or as I call it, "special knowledge," and through that gift God may show an individual something very specific about situations in other people's lives as a means to reach them.

I had a friend in Tennessee whom I dearly loved. We were always close from childhood, but when I moved to Iowa our relationship began to change. For a long time, we still had our two-hour-long phone calls to one another, but before long we were rarely talking at all.

I had no idea what was going on in her life until one day she called me, and we were talking about a mutual friend. She was telling me that he really needed prayer because his life was in a mess. At that very moment, God dropped some very specific knowledge about her into my heart. I could have never known what I was going to say to her in the next moment. I know it shocked us both, but God had revealed to me that she was the one who really needed prayer.

Not only that, but the Lord revealed to me exactly why she needed prayer. She was using drugs, and God even gave me the name of the specific drug she was using. It was a drug name that I was not even familiar with. Before that day, I had no idea she was using drugs, but as soon as God dropped that knowledge into my heart, I knew it was true.

When I told my friend what God had shown me, she began to cry uncontrollably. She asked how I could possibly know such a thing.

I told her, "God showed me, and I had no idea before this very moment. God is surely trying to save your life from the imminent destruction that drugs will cause, or He wouldn't have revealed this to me."

She was completely shaken because she thought her secret was hidden. No one knew except her, God, and now at that very moment, me. As the Holy Spirit led me, I began to pray with her, and I encouraged her to get help to break free from her addiction.

She knew that I could have had no other way of knowing what was going on with her; after all, I lived 600 miles away. But after I spoke to her she also knew that God cared enough to give someone the knowledge of her situation in order to reach out to her in an attempt to get her to flee from that destructive behavior.

Then, there is the gift referred to as "a message of wisdom." When a person demonstrates the gift of wisdom, God may give an individual a very specific word to someone about how to handle a confusing, or troubling situation.

When I think about the gift of wisdom I always think of how King Solomon asked God for wisdom, and how God honored his request. We see evidence of this in how he handled the situation with the two prostitutes who both claimed to be the mother of the same baby (1 Kings 3:16-28). When King Solomon offered to cut the child in half and give half to each woman, it was only the real mother who cried out, *"Please, my lord, give her the living baby! Don't kill him!"* (1 Kings 3:26).

God gave Solomon special knowledge to enable him to handle the situation in such a way that the real mother would be revealed. And God, through the Holy Spirit, still distributes to people the gift of wisdom today in order to provide them with godly wisdom to address problems and difficult situations.

Because the Bible is indeed living and active, we can be assured that whenever His Word goes out, it will not return empty.[18] God speaks to us through pastors, teachers, evangelists, and other members of the Church body—all those whom God uses in the administration of the Gifts of the Holy Spirit. We are admonished in the Bible to accept those ministries.

Do not despise prophetic utterances. But examine everything carefully; hold fast to that which is good; abstain from every form of evil. (1 Thessalonians 5:20-22 NASB)

Many people struggle with accepting miraculous things, and the gifts of the Holy Spirit operate in that realm. For all the sceptics, and for all those who may question the authenticity of the gifts, or the way they are used, I simply point them to the

---

18 "As the rain and the snow come down from heaven, and do not return to it without watering the earth and making it bud and flourish, so that it yields seed for the sower and bread for the eater, so is my word that goes out from my mouth: It will not return to me empty, but will accomplish what I desire and achieve the purpose for which I sent it" (Isaiah 55:10-11).

Bible. You can and should know whether or not what is done in the name of the Holy Spirit is authentic and sanctioned by God. You need not forever be confused.

You just need to know and stay close to the Scriptures. I began this chapter by laying a foundation for knowing God's actions and recognizing His voice above all others. That foundation is the Bible. All of the ministries used by God to speak to us will have one very important thing in common; they will always line up with the Word of God—the Bible. Anything that contradicts the written Word of God is not from Him, and it should be thrown out. God will never contradict himself.

But never reject what agrees with God's Word. His voice can be trusted, and if you pay attention, you will hear it.

CHAPTER 12

HOLY SPIRIT POWER

THERE IS NO power like that held and exercised by the Holy Ghost. I had never experienced what I now know to be real power until the day I experienced it first-hand—when I was baptized in the Holy Spirit with the initial evidence of speaking in tongues that I did not learn. That power made a huge difference in my life.

I needed the power of God in my life then, and I still do today—maybe now more than ever. I was an introvert for the greater part of my life, and I'm sure I would not possess the boldness I need today to stand before people and speak to them without the power of the Holy Spirit in my life. I know that I definitely would not want to attempt it!

Acts is one of my favorite books in the Bible. It is where we learn so much about the Baptism in the Holy Spirit and find direction for where the Lord wants to lead His Church.

In the first chapter of *Acts*, in verses four through eight, we read that after Jesus rose from the grave He told His disciples to remain in Jerusalem and wait for the *gift* the Father promised. He explained to them that John baptized with water, but soon they would be baptized with the Holy Spirit (the "Holy Ghost" in the King James Version). He also told them they would receive power when the Holy Spirit came upon them, and they would be His witnesses in Jerusalem, Judea, Samaria, and to the ends of the earth.

At that point in their experience the disciples could not have understood all that Jesus was talking about; but they had faith in the Lord, and after Jesus ascended to heaven they obeyed and returned to Jerusalem to wait.

As we continue reading in chapter two of *Acts*, we read about how the Holy Spirit came and filled the whole house where they were sitting. All those gathered there were filled with the Holy Spirit and began to speak in other tongues. As we read on we soon come to my favorite part of that narrative— what happened after those who heard them all speaking in other tongues accused those spirit-filled believers of being drunk.

After the disciples were accused of hitting the bottle, Peter stood up and boldly preached one of the greatest sermons one could imagine. Yes, it was Peter—the same Peter who a short time before had denied Christ three times under the pressure of revealing his relationship with Jesus to, among others, a girl who answered the door.[19]

Peter stood before a multitude of people who had gathered because of all the commotion, and he confidently preached and proclaimed the truth about Jesus and what had happened that day. Peter was changed, and he stood unashamed to proclaim the truth before anyone there to hear. And about three thousand people came to Christ that day.[20]

The followers of Jesus continued to boldly spread the gospel message from that day forward, and their ministry was accompanied by great signs and wonders. They were filled with the *Holy Spirit Power*, and their ministry showed it. That same power is still available to Christians today, and we need it in order to do what God has called us to do.

After Peter preached that day, the people were convicted and asked him what they should do. After telling them to first repent and be baptized, Peter said:

> *"And you will receive the gift of the Holy Spirit. The promise is for you and your children and for all who are far off—for all whom the Lord our God will call".*   (Acts 2:38-39)

---

19 "Simon Peter and another disciple were following Jesus. Because this disciple was known to the high priest, he went with Jesus into the high priest's courtyard, but Peter had to wait outside at the door. The other disciple, who was known to the high priest, came back, spoke to the girl on duty there and brought Peter in. 'You aren't one of his disciples too, are you?' she asked Peter. He replied, 'I am not'" (John 18:15-17).

20 Acts 2:41.

The Word of God says the promise is for us. We are among those "far off." We are among those whom the Lord is still calling today. And we need the Holy Spirit's boldness and anointing in our lives and ministries just as the early Church did. In fact, I truly believe we need the power of the Holy Spirit today more than in any other time in history.

I believe we are very close to seeing Jesus return. We need to have the boldness to share the gospel with as many people as possible. And in this increasingly evil, violent, and chaotic world, we need the Holy Spirit's help to enable us to do the Lord's work with power and His anointing.

We read about the Holy Spirit affecting the believers in the first-century Church. But I also know what I have seen the Holy Spirit do in my own walk with God, and how He has empowered me to say and do more for Him than I ever could have imagined. I never cease to be amazed by what He accomplishes in people. That is why I am so determined to tell everyone how much they need the Holy Spirit's power at work in their own lives and encourage them to ask God to give them the gift of the Holy Spirit.

When we are baptized in the Holy Spirit, God changes us, and others will notice that change. Other people will certainly recognize the difference in us when our lives become revolutionized by the power of God.

When my daughter Haley was nine years old, she came to me and said, "Mom, I want to receive the baptism of the Holy Spirit!"

Thinking she might be a little young to fully understand what she was really saying, I questioned her about what it meant to be baptized in the Holy Spirit, and why she wanted this gift.

She looked straight at me and said, "I want to have more power to witness to people."

I knew at that point she was ready. She understood that the *gift* was about having power to reach others and boldly share the gospel. She had learned that it wasn't just about speaking in an unknown tongue; it was about having the boldness to share the life-giving news of Jesus and His sacrifice for our sins.

That night at church she went to the altar, raised her arms high, and began to worship Jesus. She asked Him to fill her with the Holy Spirit. I encouraged her to just express her love to Jesus. Sometimes we focus so much on the gift of tongues that we forget to focus on the giver of the gift. I told her not to worry about that part. I told her to just tell Jesus how much she loved Him and think about how good He was to her.

She hadn't received the gift by the time the service was over, and she was so disappointed. When we went outside and got in the car, I told her, "Haley, it's not too late. You can still worship Jesus right here in the car, and you could receive the gift even before we get home."

She raised her hands, and tears poured down her little cheeks as she just worshiped Jesus. By the time we pulled into the garage at home she was praying in tongues, and it was the sweetest sound I had ever heard. She was hungry for more of God, and she desired to be closer to Jesus. Because of her desire to serve Him in a greater way, she wanted everything the Lord had for her; and the Lord was beginning to reveal that to her.

At that time, my husband Bryan had not yet received the baptism in the Holy Spirit, so it was pretty interesting when Haley and I walked through the front door that night. She still had her hands raised and was still praying in tongues. She was crying tears of joy because she was so happy. Bryan came around the corner to see what was going on, and he just stood there in amazement, looking at Haley. I looked at him and said, "Children don't make this up. This is God!"

A couple of Sundays later he too received the baptism in the Holy Spirit. Praise the Lord!

Haley was so excited after receiving the infilling of the Holy Spirit that she wanted to tell everyone she could think of. She started calling grandparents and church friends; and then she said, "I can't wait to get to school tomorrow and tell all my friends and teachers!"

That's when I thought, "Oh NO!"

You see, our daughters, Haley and Hannah, attended a private Christian school, but the baptism in the Holy Spirit was NOT promoted at that school. I started scrambling for a way to explain to her that it might not be a good idea to spring that on them just yet. After all, we didn't want her to get expelled. I just explained to her that sometimes people believe differently than we do, and even though she certainly was not wrong, it might be best *not* to mention it just yet. I told her not to worry, though, because when the time was right, God would give her the perfect opportunity to share about the *gift*.

She agreed not to say anything at school.

A few weeks later, I had to go to the school to talk with her teacher about something. While we were talking, her teacher said, "I don't know what it is, but there seems to be something different about Haley."

She continued, "In the past few weeks I've noticed that she just seems different somehow, and I can't put my finger on what it could be. She seems to always be so happy and full of joy. And when she prays there is power in her prayers, and you can feel it!"

In my mind I thought, sarcastically, "Well thank you, God. Since I didn't allow Haley to talk about it, you are giving *me* the honor!"

I reluctantly told her, "I know you don't believe the same way we do, but three weeks ago, Haley was baptized in the Holy Spirit with the evidence of speaking in tongues. The power that you felt in her prayers, and the joy you saw on her face come from the Holy Spirit."

Before I could say another word she said, "I believe you."

I'm sure I looked shocked as she continued, saying, "Lately I have been reading Acts, and I'm not so sure I know everything there is to know about the Holy Spirit. I've been asking God to show me if this gift is for us today. I think He has given me the answer."

I didn't need to say another word, because she had witnessed firsthand the power of the Holy Spirit in Haley's life.

So many times we want to hide our beliefs because we are afraid someone will think we are strange, or even crazy, to believe that the gifts of the Holy Spirit are still active today. But I believe people really want to see something different. They want to see something real, and they want to see people who are willing to share what we have that makes us different.

People want to understand what makes Spirit-filled believers bolder and causes them to speak with more power and authority. So why should we ever try to hide the very thing that could change their lives for the better?

Now to speak to another issue for a while . . . I think there are a lot of people who, once they have received the gift of the Holy Spirit, and once they are filled and speak in tongues, think that's all that is required of them. They almost act like they have arrived at their destination. They act like they've reached the end of the road. But of course that is the wrong attitude to have.

I look at the baptism in the Holy Spirit as only a beginning (albeit a great one), a starting place, a doorway to a room full of many other wonderful gifts! The Baptism in the Holy Spirit is where our life in the Spirit begins, not where it ends. God has so much more to give us if we are willing to ask and believe, but we must first be baptized in the Holy Spirit with the initial evidence of speaking in tongues. It begins there for us just like it began there for the Lord's disciples on the Day of Pentecost.

Just imagine what the Lord could do in people's lives if we all just continued to be yielded to Him and allowed the precious Holy Spirit to continue to work in and through us as the Lord provides all of the spiritual gifts recorded in the New Testament to the Church today.

We continually need every gift God is willing to give to us in order to reach the lost and hurting people in this world today. If we are willing to ask for the gifts, He is willing to give them. Once we receive the baptism in the Holy Spirit, we begin a new phase in our relationship with God. We must not stop there and rest on what we have already received. We must move even deeper into the spiritual realm. God has more for us as He equips us and uses us in ministry.

I believe God has placed a special anointing on my life to help others receive the baptism in the Holy Spirit. As I have gone out to speak, He has led me to speak on the baptism in the Holy Spirit many times, and many believers have been filled by the Holy Spirit in those services.

I will never forget one service in particular when that happened.

I was to minister in a large church that commonly had over 1,500 people in attendance in a typical service. It seemed they had more pastors on staff at that church than my own church had attendees. I began praying hard for God to show me exactly what He wanted me to share at that upcoming speaking engagement.

To say the least, I was very intimidated. I was especially concerned because of what I knew about all of the knowledge, degrees, seminary, and years of experience some of those pastors had under their belt. And there I was, only a Certified Minister[21] with a limited amount of Bible school behind me.

As the date of my opportunity to minister approached, I started asking God why He had even put me in that situation. I began to point out to Him that their pastors had far more knowledge and experience than I, and I was certain I could never share with the congregation anything they hadn't already heard a thousand times and with far more eloquence than I could ever say it.

Then it was as if God simply whispered into my heart, "Are you willing to look foolish for me?"

I had to stop and think about that for a moment. I had been so worried about what these people were going to think about me and how I presented the message that I had taken my eyes off the simple message God intended for me to share.

As I looked down at the Bible I had just opened in my lap, these are the words that jumped off the pages at me:

For the foolishness of God is wiser than human wisdom, and the weakness of God is stronger than human strength. Brothers

---

21 Certified Minister—the first level of ministerial credentials in the Assemblies of God.

and sisters, think of what you were when you were called. Not many of you were wise by human standards; not many were influential; not many were of noble birth. But God chose the foolish things of the world to shame the wise; God chose the weak things of the world to shame the strong. God chose the lowly things of this world and the despised things—and the things that are not—to nullify the things that are, so that no one may boast before him. (1 Corinthians 1:25-29)

Then, before I could even form a decent argument to what I'd read (about how that could apply to me in my situation), God immediately led me right across the page to:

And so it was with me, brothers and sisters. When I came to you, I did not come with eloquence or human wisdom as I proclaimed to you the testimony about God. For I resolved to know nothing while I was with you except Jesus Christ and him crucified. I came to you in weakness with great fear and trembling. My message and my preaching were not with wise and persuasive words, but with a demonstration of the Spirit's power, so that your faith might not rest on human wisdom, but on God's power. (1 Corinthians 2:1-5)

Wow! Did I ever relate with Paul in those words!

I can promise you that as I stood before that large congregation, I had no eloquent words, or great wisdom; but what I *did* have more than made up for it. The Lord allowed me to go there with a demonstration of the Holy Spirit's power. And that didn't happen just because God had saved this terrible sinner and completely turned her life around (although that was where it started). And it didn't happen just because I had come to the realization that God could take a total introvert and give her a voice to speak the Word of God boldly to so many people.

It happened because I put my complete trust in Him for that service and allowed the power of the Holy Spirit to work in and through me. It happened because I was willing to look foolish if necessary in order to bring Him glory. And it happened because I was content to speak the messages of the Cross and the Baptism in the Holy Spirit in all their simplicity.

Jesus walked into that sanctuary, and He saved people and baptized hundreds in the Holy Spirit that morning.

Sometimes we make things so difficult. We don't need to make it so hard. We just need to have childlike faith and believe we can have what He has promised us. We desperately need the power of the Holy Spirit in our lives.

As I close this chapter, I want to make it clear that I am not against academics. I'm not against studying and learning all we can. I agree we must study to show ourselves approved by God.[22] We must know the Bible and understand what we are talking about. But we must never become so reliant on our own qualifications, our levels of learning, our knowledge, or our experience and fleshly understanding, that we neglect giving the Holy Spirit the privilege and the room to simply move through us and among us.

---

22 "Study to shew thyself approved unto God, a workman that needeth not to be ashamed, rightly dividing the word of truth" (2 Timothy 2:15 KJV).

Seek God if you desire to have the gifts, the ministries of the Holy Spirit, active in your life. Ask Him for the *leading gift*—the baptism in the Holy Spirit—the gift through which the others operate, and around which they all revolve. He wants you to have this gift more than you want to receive it. You can be certain of that!

Allow God to baptize you in the Holy Spirit. Then allow Him to keep you full to overflowing. My prayer is for you to experience the *Holy Spirit Power* in your life and witness.

CHAPTER 13

THE VALLEY OF DOUBT

I WISH I COULD say that I have never had a single doubt about my calling from the very first day I realized God called me into ministry. Unfortunately, that has not been the case. I've had all kinds of doubts. (I expand on "doubt" from chapters 3 and 4.)

When I used to read about the Israelites in the Bible—how God parted the Red Sea and allowed them to walk through on dry ground, for instance—I wondered in my mind how anyone could be so crazy as to doubt God concerning anything after witnessing His miracles.

I always wanted to ask them, "How about the manna from Heaven, or the water gushing out of a rock? How much proof do you need before you can depend on God in every circumstance?"

Then I was called into ministry, and soon I realized I had no right to look down on their lack of faith at all. I myself have seen God do miraculous things. I have had Him answer prayers in such ways that there was no denying it was His power alone that brought them about. But I've experienced success one week, and the very next week I have felt like I was in a pit of darkness with no escape!

The truth is, we are human; and as such, it should be no surprise that we find ourselves dealing with doubts and struggling with maintaining faith from time to time. I believe we will have less doubt and more faith in our lives as we grow in our relationship with the Lord. But I don't think we will ever be totally free from occasionally dealing with doubts as long as we live in these earthly vessels. (But that is clearly my opinion. I guess I shouldn't speak for you.)

I didn't realize how difficult it can be sometimes for believers who are called into a ministry to drown out the enemy's attempts to influence them and try to convince them they are not actually called by God—or that God is finished with them. As I continue in this chapter let me make clear that I *now* know beyond a shadow of a doubt that God did call me to do what I'm doing.

But I admit that I am still sometimes tempted with various doubts and lack of confidence. It hasn't been that long since I was walking through my own valley of doubt. In that valley I felt like I had just spoken for my very last congregation. I thought God was probably finished with me and would never use me again.

I was invited to speak at a women's conference at a very large church one time on a Saturday, and I was very excited. Then the Pastor decided to ask me to speak for all three services that Sunday as well. I agreed to it, and I was thrilled.

As I was seeking God and trying to prepare for the upcoming services, it was as if the Lord simply whispered to me, "I am going to call someone into ministry Sunday, and I want you to confirm it to him." It was the first time God had ever revealed something to me before I even arrived at the venue.

At first I questioned, "God, was that really you?" In that next second, an image of a young black man popped into my head. He was clean shaven and had no hair at all on his head. He wore round glasses with thin rims. He was very slim, and he was wearing a light blue shirt. He had a warm smile and a very pleasant demeanor. That image never left my mind. I confided in a few friends what God had shown me, and I even described the young man to them.

God led me to speak about the Baptism in the Holy Spirit that Sunday morning, so that is exactly what I did. And I was amazed to see how the Lord moved in the service. It was a large church, but even so, it was amazing to see hundreds of people come to the altar.

The power and presence of God seemed to just sweep through the congregation that morning as many believers were baptized in the Holy Spirit. It was a beautiful sight and sound! I couldn't wait to get off the platform and go among the people to help pray with them. I handed the service back over to the pastor and walked off the platform. I could barely squeeze through the crowd as they stood—hands raised high—crying out to God for more. It was overwhelming.

The church had a prayer team, and they were praying with many. I had no idea who was on the prayer team and who wasn't, so I just began to squeeze through the people until I felt like God would have me pray for someone. Before I knew it, I was on the opposite side of the church from where I started.

I was just about to turn to go back the other way when I looked to my right, and there was the young man God had shown me! (I had totally forgotten about what God had spoken to me until that very instant.) Every detail of the man's appearance was the same as in the vision God had given me.

I stepped forward and asked him, "Young man, do you know that God has called you into ministry?"

He looked at me with a surprised expression, and then tears began to well up in his eyes and trickle down his face. He said, "I don't know, but I think so."

I told him, "Yes you have been called, and God sent me here to confirm to you that He has called you." I prayed for him and then made my way back through the crowd.

Soon the service ended, and I was surrounded by people who wanted to talk to me. And at the very back of the crowd stood the young man. He waited patiently, and when we finally sat down together, he said, "I have gone through Bible College and completed all the requirements to be a minister, but I just had so many doubts in myself—and no open doors—so I gave up."

"I want to be like you," he continued. "You preached and was certain that God was going to move, and He did. You didn't even know me, or that God had called me into ministry, but you boldly proclaimed it to me. I want to be *that* way. I don't want to have any doubts."

With sincerest empathy, I said to him, "Good luck with that!"

I then shared with him that I am constantly doubting myself. I told him that while I believe God is always capable of moving powerfully in a service, I understand that He may choose not to do so.

I said, "After God moves in a miraculous way, I often leave the service on *cloud nine*—so excited. But the following week I might be found hiding in a cave somewhere like Elijah— doubting myself more than ever and feeling so depressed that I'm almost tempted to throw in the towel."

He thought I was joking, but I told him I was being completely honest.

I didn't want to discourage the young man, but I *did* want him to realize that our callings cannot be based on feelings, alone. Just as our salvation must not be based on our feelings— it is based on the Word of God, our faith in Jesus Christ, His sacrifice on the Cross, His death, and His resurrection—so also must our response to God's callings for our lives not be dependent on human feelings.[23]

---

23 Human feelings are tricky things. The devil knows that, and he and his minions continually attempt to play on our feelings to convince us to give up anything we are doing that brings value to the Kingdom. We must not allow Satan to have his way with our feelings. We must stand in faith against him.

I encouraged the young man the best I could, and I told him how God had even shown me a picture of him before I came to that church to enable me to recognize him and tell him God called him to minister. Then he told me something that added to our amazement. He told me he didn't even attend that church. He and his wife were just visiting.

God knows where to find us!

As the experience of that young man illustrates, our doubts can trip us up. The temptation to doubt can be powerful. Anytime we face the temptation to doubt God's calls and intentions for us, we must rise above our feelings and face every situation with faith and trust in God. He calls us not only to our ministries but also to the Cross. We must take our doubts to the Cross, trust what the Lord has already spoken to us, and rely on Him to bring victories in our lives both today and in the future just like He has done in the past.

I spoke on healing that same night, and many were healed in the service. I was so excited that I could barely contain myself because of the awe and wonder of what God had done—and the fact that He would even allow me to be involved in it. I couldn't have been happier, and I was ready to go out again and see God do even greater things somewhere else.

Then . . .

Two weeks later I sat in my prayer room staring at the wall and wondering if God had abandoned me. I know it sounds ridiculous, but it was anything but that to me. I had no speaking engagements in the near future. In fact, I had only one lined up for the whole remainder of the year—and it was only April.

It seemed like every door to speak was closed and locked. I began asking myself why God was putting me on the bench after He had done such great things at my last speaking event. "Was that my *last* speaking engagement? Is God already finished with me? Have I done something wrong?"

Thousands of questions raced through my mind as I sought to understand. Over and over I thought, "Why, why, why?"

Discouragement swept in, and I became depressed. I prayed and prayed and prayed, but it seemed like the more I prayed the less I could feel God's presence. I still worshipped Him and tried to maintain a "happy face," but on the inside I was sitting in that cave right next to Elijah.[24]

Considering my past experiences, one wouldn't think I would be surprised at that point. After all, I already knew that the big mountaintop events in my life were often followed by valleys. But for me, this particular valley of doubt was extremely dark.

When we don't see God moving in our situations, or when we don't see God opening doors for us in our timing, we can begin to get discouraged and doubt that we are walking in His will. But we can't give up in those situations. God is faithful. He keeps His promises, and He does not change His mind after He calls us.[25]

---

24 Read about Elijah's experience in 1 Kings, chapter nineteen.
25 "For God's gifts and his call are irrevocable" (Romans 11:29).

Our Lord may change the direction of our callings, but He does not change His mind about calling us to ministry. And that makes sense because He already knew everything about us when He appointed us to our work in the first place. Before God called us, He already knew how we would respond to His directions, and He knew what our responses would be to the challenges we would face.

God knew that I would struggle many times with doubt over my calling, and yet He still wanted me to do a work for Him. That in itself is encouraging to me, and it is one of those things that continues to allow me to rise above my feelings in faith and continue to do His will.

I've had other ministers prophesy over me and tell me about things that God has in store for me. I have felt the Lord's presence to confirm many of those words, and I knew in those times that they were speaking from the heart of God. Some of the things spoken over me have come to pass, and some have not yet been fulfilled.

I don't always know God's timing, but here is one thing I do know: I know He is not finished with me. I know this because I know the Lord is true to His word. I believe I will see the Lord's will come to pass, and I choose to trust Him to be in control of the timing.

I speak of these things from experience, and I have confidence that the Lord wants me to use these words in sharing my experiences with you. This is to encourage and bless you in your Christian walk and ministry.

As I look back at all the times I've been in spiritual valleys (and I take no pride in saying that the land of doubt is not new territory to me), I say with joy that God has never failed to bring me out of those experiences. But while I recognize it was only because of the power and faithfulness of God that I was able to be released from the darkness in those valleys, I also understand that I had a part to play in those releases.

When we are struggling with doubt and discouragement, we ourselves will make decisions that either release God's power to change our circumstances or drive us farther away from His will and deeper into the darkness of doubt.

When struggling through those challenging days, I was able to rise above my feelings because I refused to trust in the finality of my emotions. I made a conscious decision to move forward. I decided to never give in to my feelings at the cost of failing to trust in God to lead me and prepare my path.

Instead of succumbing to continually living in discouragement, I decided to maintain my belief and trust in God's love for me and His ability to lead. And I decided to maintain my faith and trust in Him until I was out of the valley and once again climbing toward my next mountaintop experience.

God responds to the faith and trust we put in Him. He knows our human tendencies. He knows our weaknesses. He knows how to deal with us, and certainly there is no shortage of His ability to bring us through all the challenges we face. Also, there is no limit to His capacity to teach us valuable lessons through all of life's experiences.

And remember this: God is no respecter of persons. Just as He will save anyone who repents and comes to Him, He will never stop His work in us after He has saved us and called us into His work.

The Holy Spirit will never stop sanctifying, discipling, and empowering God's children. That's because we are the ones the Lord appointed to make up His Church—the body of Christ.[26] He is doing those things for me now, and He will do them in the future. He is doing those things for others, too. And He will do them for you if your response to God continues to be one inspired by faith and trust.

If you find yourself in a valley of doubt and discouragement, you must believe God and trust Him to bring you through it.

Here is how I often handle my own times of doubt and depression:

First, I ask myself, "What can I learn while I'm here? (I certainly won't learn anything from the experience if I spend all my time pouting.) I look back on the victories God has given me in the past and all the wonderful things He has done so far in my life and ministry. Then I reflect on His faithfulness, and I choose to believe God's best for me is yet to come if I remain faithful to Him. Next, I choose to stand on God's Word and believe the Lord

---

26 "Now you are the body of Christ, and each one of you is a part of it"
   (1 Corinthians 12:27).

has a good plan that He is working out in my life even if that plan involves present pain—or even correction.[27]

If you are traveling through a time of doubt or depression, and if you are tempted to throw in the towel, don't do it. (Ultimately God gives you the choice.) Understand that a visit in the valley of discouragement and doubt is not all that uncommon in Christian ministry—regardless of the type of ministry. It's not pleasant in that valley, but we must remember that God does not leave us alone there. The Holy Spirit is there with us to guide and counsel us.

For me now, it's not usually wondering if I will survive the ordeal that bothers me the most, but it's the act of simply waiting to get out of the emotional valleys I experience that is often the most difficult part. I'll be the first to admit that I've never been a very patient person, so I often become even more discouraged when I must wait for any significant period of time.

As I wait I am sometimes tempted to try to "help myself" out of a valley without trusting in and allowing God to bring about

---

27 The prophet Jeremiah delivered a word from the Lord to the citizens of the land of Judah. Even though their future was to be filled with many more years of suffering because of God's judgment upon their nation, God still had a plan for them—a plan that would bring them future blessings.

"This is what the Lord says: 'When seventy years are completed for Babylon, I will come to you and fulfill my good promise to bring you back to this place. For I know the plans I have for you,' declares the Lord, 'plans to prosper you and not to harm you, plans to give you hope and a future. Then you will call on me and come and pray to me, and I will listen to you. You will seek me and find me when you seek me with all your heart'" (Jeremiah 29:10-13).

His perfect solution. Helping myself out of valley experiences without waiting for God's will to be accomplished has not always yielded the best results.

If we don't take the time to learn what we need to learn in a valley that the Lord allows us to go through, and if our valley experience has not increased our faith in the Lord, we shouldn't be surprised to soon find ourselves challenged and once again no better equipped to deal with doubt or handle discouragement than we were in the past.

Sometimes God requires us to wait in the valleys for a while, and it feels absolutely excruciating to do it. But if you are in a valley now, you may as well use your time there constructively.

Look around you. Decide what you can do while you're there. Ask yourself what God may be trying to show you or teach you through the experience. Is there another area of your life that God wants you to focus on while there? Is the Lord trying to redirect or expand your ministry or the influence you have in a different way? Has the Lord allowed your valley experience to continue longer because He wants you to fill a season just spending quality time with HIM?

Our valley experiences can end up fostering enormous blessings and Christian growth in us. But it depends on how we respond to them.

Don't sit down and close your eyes in frustration when dealing with doubt. Don't give up in discouragement. Don't quit!

Look for truth and value in the valleys. With your experiences there properly handled, you can leave the valleys with greater faith and stronger resolve.

And by the way, don't despair over the missing view from the mountaintop. Before you know it, you will be up there again.

CHAPTER 14

I'M GOING TO JAIL

I COULD TELL you story after story to illustrate how God's timing is always best and how He knows exactly what He's doing. In fact, I think the majority of this book probably reiterates that message very well. The story I am about to relate to you just happens to be another instance when something I really wanted to work just wouldn't work at all, but through this experience the Lord reinforced to me His ability to lead and direct.

A few years ago, when I lived in Iowa, I was leading a women's group in my home church, and I loved it. At the time, I was speaking for the women's group in the church once a month and hadn't even considered speaking outside my own church. However, I felt like I could be doing more.

"But what could that be?" I wondered.

Without going into a lot of detail, let me just say that I decided—with a little nudge from the Holy Spirit—that I wanted to get involved in jail or prison ministry to women prisoners.

I started calling prisons and jails to see what I would need to do to get in to speak to the women. After a few phone calls it was quite evident that it was not going to be easy—if even possible. I started to think the only way I could get into jail would be to rob a bank. (But I guess that would kinda negate my testimony, wouldn't it?)

Still, I completed all the forms that were sent to me by the officials of one jail to start the process of gaining standing for ministry to prisoners, sent them back, and waited—and waited. I started calling every week to see if there were things I could do to speed up the process; but no, there wasn't. The place was on lockdown—literally!

However, in just a few weeks my family and my whole world seemed to flip upside down, and suddenly, God was moving us back to Tennessee. Jail ministry obviously was the last thing on my mind at that point.

I felt like a fish out of water when we arrived in Tennessee. I couldn't figure out why on earth God would move us back when everything was going so well in Iowa. We came to love our church and church family while in Iowa. The girls attended a great Christian school, where they were happy. We lived in a great neighborhood with wonderful neighbors and friends. I wondered why God would uproot us and move us to Tennessee.

To top it all off, when we started looking for a church in Tennessee, we just didn't feel like we fit in anywhere. We visited many churches that we liked, but none of them felt like *home*. We searched for a home church for almost two years before we finally chose the right one.

After being in that church for three or four months, I began to hear things about a women's jail ministry—nothing real specific, but I heard the church had one. I didn't give it another thought, though, because I had tried to get in that door in Iowa, and it just didn't work out. I pretty much dismissed it from my mind.

"It probably isn't my calling anyway," I thought "so why bother with it now?"

While attending our new church in Tennessee I was asked by the women's leader to speak for her women's group, and I agreed to do it. After the meeting was over, I thought it went horribly wrong. I felt like all the women were bored to death. I even noticed one lady fiddling with her cell phone the entire time I was speaking. Needless to say, I was so disappointed!

After dropping off my friend at her house, I pretty much cried all the way home. I had never felt so terrible after speaking. I was discouraged, and I started feeling like anything I put my hand to do in Tennessee would be a complete failure.

I wondered, "What in the world am I doing here anyway?"

I began to really relate to the words of Jesus, when He said, *"A prophet is not without honor, but in his own country, and among his own kin, and in his own house"* (Mark 6:4 KJV).

There I was, back in the state where I was born and raised, and it seemed like I was completely invisible. Very few pastors in Tennessee invited me to come and minister in the churches they pastored, and when someone did, it seemingly resulted in what I would call a small disaster. But I had already been given the opportunity by that time to minister to women's groups in other states, and when I ministered in other states God showed up in amazing ways. People were saved, healed, and baptized in the Holy Spirit in those places; yet I felt totally worthless in my own home state.

Before long the Holy Spirit began to bring back to my remembrance the jail ministry that I had once been interested in developing. Initially, though, I tried to ignore it because I didn't think it was a good time to undertake the responsibility. I was traveling and ministering in other states, writing a book, and counseling people on a daily basis. I didn't really have time to work jail ministry into my schedule. Besides, I thought it would have been much better if God had opened the prison's doors to me before now, so I dismissed the idea.

But, God is persistent when He wants us to do something. I eventually began feeling convicted about my lack of interest in the very ministry that I previously strongly felt God wanted me to be involved in. So after feeling horrible conviction for quite some time about not being fully obedient to God, I approached my pastor and told him I would like to help out with the jail ministry if possible. He told me he would tell Sarah, the lady in charge of the women's jail ministry, to contact me.

I didn't know her, and I didn't hear anything back from her immediately; so I said, "OK God, I tried, and it didn't work out. I've done my part."

Of course the next day after saying that, Sarah called and was bubbling with excitement. She said, "We have got to talk!

Meet me at the diner for lunch." We met, and I was certainly not prepared to hear what she was going to tell me.

We began our chat by sharing our testimonies with each other. Then she told me, "I know you are the one who is supposed to come and take over the jail ministry."

My jaw must have hit the floor as she explained to me that she and her husband were planning to move, and she had been praying desperately for someone to come in and take over.

She said, "I can still tell you what you were wearing the first day you walked into our church, because that was the day God said to me, 'That's her!' I didn't know anything else about you, but I knew what God said to me."

"As I continued to pray, God told me not to approach you but to continue praying and trusting that He would have you come to me—and He did!"

At that point I thought, "This is just *not* a good time; perhaps God has someone else who can do a better job."

I entertained myself with countless other excuses, as well. But deep down I knew I was experiencing another divine encounter. She wanted me to speak to the ladies in the jail as soon as possible, and I was excited to meet them.

But speaking to the ladies in the jail proved to be a little more difficult than expected. When I arrived I was told that I could not go in and speak to anyone without taking a class. I asked when the classes would be held, and the deputy gave me a very vague answer, which I interpreted as, "I don't know, and I don't care."

Once again I began to think this was just another failed attempt to do anything in Tennessee! It looked like no ministry opportunities in my state of residence were going to open up.

I finally prayed and just said, "God, only you know whether or not you want me to do this. If you want me to do it, please work it out, and if not, just close the door."

About a week later Sarah called and said, "I need you to go to the jail. They have a sign-up sheet for that class!"

After her call, I went to the jail and signed up, and a week later I completed the jail class that would allow me to minister in any jail in the state of Tennessee.

I must admit, after taking the class and hearing about all the things that *could happen*, I did have some uneasy thoughts about being locked in a room behind a steel door with a bunch of inmates. But I soon realized that we had a lot in common. You see, when I walked away from God all those years ago, I was doing things they had done (and probably more than some of those ladies who were sitting in that room). The difference was, I didn't get caught.

I was a little nervous the first time I went into the jail, but I was going into that room with a heart full of love—not just my own love but the perfect love of Christ. I considered myself simply His hands and feet.

There were two ladies in the room when I walked in, and one of them said, "You've got your job cut out for you today! We've got some ladies in here who are probably going to be pretty rough. They may walk around and talk and curse, and they probably won't pay attention to a word you say; but please don't get discouraged. Please come back again no matter what they do."

Hearing that was a little unsettling to say the least. The deputy had explained to me that if anything happened, I could knock on the window, and they would come to my aid. However, that window was about twenty feet from where I was standing, and that wasn't real comforting.

Soon there were eight ladies sitting around a table with me, and I started speaking to them by introducing myself. Then I told them that no one in that room had done anything worse than I had done.

"The truth is," I told them, "even if I had accepted Christ as my Savior at 5 years old, and even if I had walked faithfully with Him ever since that day, the spiritual application behind that statement would still be true, because we are all born in sin, and one sin is just as black as any other before God."

"But unfortunately, that certainly wasn't the case with me," I said. "I have faltered along the way."

I poured out to them an account of my own sinful past. And not one of the women got out of her seat; not one interrupted or said anything. I then began to share how I came to my senses, like the prodigal son,[28] and how I ran to the altar and asked Jesus to forgive me. As I looked around the room the ladies were wiping away tears from their eyes. There was such a sweet presence of the Holy Spirit in that small room, and soon I asked if anyone would like to ask Jesus to be her Savior.

Three women gave their lives to Christ that morning, and then I, too, was wiping tears from my eyes.

Jail ministry has certainly been a unique experience, but those ladies have become so special to me. When I'm with them, I never let them leave that room without giving them a great big hug and telling them I love them. I pray for them throughout the week, and I want the best for each one of them. I feel blessed to have the privilege of experiencing Jesus loving them through me.

Though I may have felt like Tennessee was just a bad place for me in ministry, God knew all along what He had planned for me there. And like I said, He knows how to lead and direct us, and He will. That is, He will lead anyone who desires to follow Him. It turned out that the doors of ministry I found closed to me simply served to draw my attention to other areas of needed ministry. I still travel as an evangelist ministering in other states, but I now feel confident that there is always something of value to the Kingdom that I can do when I'm not traveling.

Sometimes when ministry opportunities are not obvious to believers who want to be busy about the Lord's work to which they feel called, there are other avenues of ministry that God is

---

28 Read the story Jesus told about the prodigal son in Luke 15:11-32.   .

trying to show us. But perhaps we are too prone to make the mistake of dismissing His direction, and thinking, "I don't feel like God is calling me to do that."

We should not be so shortsighted.

A sweet friend once asked me, "Are you sure God is calling you to do jail ministry?" I admit I had my doubts many times about that along the way, and I asked myself that same question. But then I remembered these words of Jesus in Matthew:

Then the King will say to those on his right, "Come, you who are blessed by my Father; take your inheritance, the kingdom prepared for you since the creation of the world. For I was hungry and you gave me something to eat, I was thirsty and you gave me something to drink, I was a stranger and you invited me in, I needed clothes and you clothed me, I was sick and you looked after me, I was in prison and you came to visit me."

Then the righteous will answer him, "Lord, when did we see you hungry and feed you, or thirsty and give you something to drink? When did we see you a stranger and invite you in, or needing clothes and clothe you? When did we see you sick or in prison and go to visit you?"

The King will reply, "Truly I tell you, whatever you did for one of the least of these brothers and sisters of mine, you did for me." (Matthew 25:34-40)

There may be times when we feel like we can't do anything of value in ministry because of our location, our circumstances, our lack of knowledge, or our experience; but that's not true. Some of us may feel like God hasn't called us to do anything that we believe is significant, so we hesitate to step out to do anything. But God does not call all of us to high-profile ministries (if that's what we think of as "significant").

Some ministries may seem more important than others to us, but they aren't. Regardless of what we think of the size or notoriety of ministries, we do well to remind ourselves—and each other—that the most important ministries are simply those through which the needs of the *least of these* are met.

When it comes right down to basics, our location, experience, money, and education should have nothing to do with how we view our need to be involved in reaching out to others. As the redeemed, we all have a story of hope to tell, and we have a responsibility to represent Christ in the world. We don't always need to wait until we *feel called* before we take action to share what we have in Christ. God has already asked all of us to represent Him to the lost and those in need.

I'm going to jail. Where are you going? The blessings and love you will receive by sharing the Good News with others, and the joy you will share by serving God, will be greater than any experience you have known. Look around you today. Who are the *least of these* near you?

CHAPTER 15

THE "H" WORD

UNFORTUNATELY, SOME MEMBERS of my extended family are non-believers. On one particular occasion, I invited one of my relatives to go to church with us. She responded to me by saying that she had no reason to go to church because most of the people sitting in the pews were doing things that were *much* worse than anything she had ever done.

She asked, "So why would I want to go sit in a room with a bunch of hypocrites?" (That, my friend, is the "H" word.)

I must admit, her answer caught me off guard at first. But I looked at her and gently replied, "One day you will answer to God, not to the people sitting in the pews. And all of them will also answer to God for themselves. We don't go to church to seek imperfect people; we go to seek God, who is perfect in all of His ways."

She continued to ramble on about how she wasn't a hypocrite, so she wasn't going to go to church and pretend to be someone she was not. I soon realized that trying to convince her she should view things differently was a battle I was not going to win. She had made up her mind.

It seems many people like to use that same excuse for not attending church. And that's too bad. We need to find a way to reach them. But the most effective way, of course, would be to make sure we ourselves avoid hypocrisy like the plague. We need to get rid of it anywhere it exists. It has no place in the Lord's Church.

I'm sure many of us know people who truly are hypocrites— or at least those who struggle with hypocritical attitudes. People with hypocritical spirits can really do a lot of damage to those who are sincerely trying to serve God, and they can give to non-believers the excuses they need to live their lives apart from Christ.

It is critically important for believers to walk out their faith with humility, sincerity, and honesty. And we must be vigilant to not look upon others with condemnation in our hearts, because a condemning spirit is one of the main ingredients in the recipe for making a hypocrite.

People don't like hypocrisy, nor should they.

Jesus called the Pharisees hypocrites. He did that because He detested the way they practiced their faith. And when He did so, He used strong words:

> *"Woe to you, teachers of the law and Pharisees, you hypocrites!*
> *You are like whitewashed tombs, which look beautiful on the*

outside but on the inside are full of the bones of the dead and everything unclean. In the same way, on the outside you appear to people as righteous but on the inside you are full of hypocrisy and wickedness."   (Matthew 23:27-28)

The Pharisees gave the impression to everyone that they had it all together. They were the ones who had conquered sin to such degree that they could lord it over others who were not so successful. To them, they were the authorities on how to live a holy life, and no one should question them on their standing with God.

But Jesus knew better. Jesus knew they were simply judgmental hypocrites. We can all come to agreement with the Lord and support what He thought of the Pharisees; but if we're not careful, some of us could come to reflect some of the same attitudes they had. We need to avoid adopting the judgmental attitudes of the Pharisees—those attitudes revealed to us in the New Testament. Attitudes like theirs will have a terrible effect on our abilities to show love and compassion to others.

None of us are perfect; we all mess up, and we all have our faults and weaknesses. But unlike people who just struggle sometimes in dealing with their weaknesses, hypocrites ignore their condition and try to rationalize that if they have sins, their sins are somehow *cleaner* or not as bad as the sins others have committed.

But tell me, where does anyone get any biblical support for forming such an attitude? All sin warrants repentance. All sin makes us unclean, and the only thing that can cleanse us of any sin is the precious blood of Jesus!

One of the things I have struggled with in jail ministry is the rigid feelings the ladies have about attending church when they finally get out of jail. Many of them feel that if they attend church they will be looked down upon, or judged. They think people will hold their past sins against them or refuse to believe they have changed. In their minds they imagine people whispering about them and pointing fingers.

Unfortunately, their fears are all too often justified, because there are some people in churches whose hypocritical spirits cause them to react that way to people whose lives have not measured up to their standards. I have spent a lot of time trying to show the ladies in jail that God looks on the heart, while man looks at our appearances.[29] God knows us inside and out; and our love for Him, and the desires of our hearts to serve Him, are what He values above all.

Many of these jail-ladies have tattoos and piercings all over. They usually don't wear fancy dresses and six-inch heels. They usually don't have beautiful, well-maintained hairstyles. And most of the time they attend church just as they are—in jeans, T-shirts, or sweat suits. They go into a church where other people wear expensive dresses, jewelry, shoes, suits, and ties; and there are instances when those well-dressed people do, in fact, have a tendency to look down on these ladies.

---

29 "But the Lord said to Samuel, 'Do not consider his appearance or his height, for I have rejected him. The Lord does not look at the things people look at. People look at the outward appearance, but the Lord looks at the heart'" (1 Samuel 16:7).

Sometimes people will avoid others who don't meet their standards, and they will stare at them from a distance with thoughts of disgust displayed all over their faces. Let me just say this: You can be dressed to the hilt and be drop-dead gorgeous on the outside, but if you have a hypocritical attitude, that attitude reveals what is inside you just as the attitudes of the Pharisees revealed what they really were. To put it into plain English, nothing is uglier than snobby, self-righteous hypocrites! They are like whitewashed tombs.

I have shared my testimony all over the nation with all kinds of congregations. I try to be as transparent as I can about my ugly past when I share with others what the Lord has done for me. I'm not proud of my past, so I don't talk about it for any other reason than to encourage people to believe that God can bring beauty from ashes. God has honored my intentions, and I'm always amazed at how the Holy Spirit uses my testimony to minister to people and touch their lives for His Kingdom.

I'm always overwhelmed by the responses of people to my testimony. And I'm amazed at how many people come to me after services and share their own stories of failure, and of God's redeeming grace in their lives. I've had many people tell me they have been ashamed to tell others about their own past failures because they were afraid of what people would think of them.

They tell me they were afraid of being judged by others. But when they see what God can do through a person who is transparent when giving testimony to what God can do with a wrecked life—through a person whose only reason for doing so is giving the glory to God—they too are encouraged to go out and share their stories with others.

Testimonies of God's power and goodness need to be published. People need to hear what God does! We need not be ashamed to give glory to God for what He has done and point others to Him for solutions to their problems. All through the ages people have been relieved to find out that God loves them in their broken conditions and desires to bring healing and deliverance to them. People are thrilled to see that God can and does use people with broken pasts.

However, on one occasion I was asked to speak for a women's meeting and share my testimony, and I found a quite different response from the women in that meeting.

As I began to share my story, I could almost feel the disdain for me in that room. To me the feeling was absolutely tangible. The atmosphere in that place seemed to completely stifle the anointing of the Holy Spirit.

As I looked out over the crowd, I had an overwhelming sense that they felt I was unworthy to speak to them. It occurred to me that perhaps they felt I would get them dirty since I had such an imperfect past. As I poured my heart out to them with as much honesty and transparency as I could muster, I began to feel embarrassed and hurt.

No one responded to the altar call. The ladies seemed to huddle in their own little groups when the meeting was over. And whether they were or not, I felt they were criticizing me. I felt totally humiliated, and I vowed to never speak for that group again (though I was sure I wouldn't be asked back, anyway).

As I look back on how I was hurt by their attitudes and actions, I realize that Jesus was likely hurt as well. You see, Jesus died and poured out His precious blood to cover all our sins— my sins, their sins, and your sins. The Lord doesn't go around considering my sins, or anyone's sins, dirtier than others. And it must grieve the Lord so terribly when some of the people He died for look upon others, for whom He also died, with disdain and disrespect.

I am not saying all those ladies I ministered to were hypocrites, but the way of hypocrisy is surely paved with the feelings I sensed in the place where we were gathered.

Although some sins may be more hideous or egregious than others, sins are sins. And Jesus died to forgive us and deliver us from all of them. He chose to die for us long before He ascended the Cross.[30] Even when God created us He knew we would all make mistakes, and although some of our mistakes can seem hundreds of times worse than others, we are all dirty and undone without Him. Jesus died for us knowing that some would never

---

30 "All inhabitants of the earth will worship the beast—all whose names have not been written in the Lamb's book of life, the Lamb that was slain from the creation of the world" (Revelation 13:8).

even appreciate or accept His gift of forgiveness, but He still willingly laid down His life for us all.

> *Very rarely will anyone die for a righteous man; though for a good person someone might possibly dare to die. But God demonstrates His own love for us in this: while we were yet sinners, Christ died for us.* (Romans 5:7-8)

Paul was the writer of those words. Take note that Paul used the word "we" when he talked about who the sinners had been. Paul had a lot to be ashamed of when it comes to the way he lived his life before accepting Christ. His sins were B-A-D! Before becoming a Christian, Paul fought against the Lord and His Church as hard, or even harder perhaps, than any enemy of the Cross today fights against the standards held by today's Church.

Paul (whose name had been Saul) was implicated in the death of Stephen, the first Christian martyr.

> *When the members of the Sanhedrin heard this, they were furious and gnashed their teeth at him. But Stephen, full of the Holy Spirit, looked up to heaven and saw the glory of God, and Jesus standing at the right hand of God.*
>
> *"Look," he said, "I see heaven open and the Son of Man standing at the right hand of God."*
>
> *At this they covered their ears and, yelling at the top of their voices, they all rushed at him, dragged him out of the city and began to stone him. Meanwhile, the witnesses laid their coats at the feet of a young man named Saul.*

*While they were stoning him, Stephen prayed, "Lord Jesus,
receive my spirit." Then he fell on his knees and cried out,
"Lord, do not hold this sin against them." When he had said this,
he fell asleep.*

And Saul approved of their killing him.　　(Acts 7:54-8:1a)

Paul became a destroyer of the Lord's Church after Stephen's
death. He made it his mission, and the Jewish leaders promoted
his actions as he went from city to city, and house to house, to
arrest Christians and have them thrown into prison.

*On that day a great persecution broke out against the church in
Jerusalem, and all except the apostles were scattered throughout
Judea and Samaria. Godly men buried Stephen and mourned
deeply for him. But Saul began to destroy the church. Going
from house to house, he dragged off men and women and put
them in prison.*　　(Acts 8:1b-3)

But Paul met Jesus one day on the road to Damascus, and his
life was changed. (Read Acts chapter nine.)

After accepting Jesus as his personal savior, after he had been
delivered from the bondage of sin, it was time for Paul to join the
Church in fellowship. It was time for him to begin meeting with
fellow Christians on a regular basis and minister alongside them.
Inevitably, though, other Christians were hesitant to trust Paul.

They may not have seen any marks in his person. They
certainly would not have been able to tell by the way he dressed
that he had a different or troubled past compared to their own.
But they knew what he had been, and that is what troubled them.

Similar to what happens in churches today, some people were slower to accept Paul into fellowship than others, but he *was* accepted. He was given a chance to prove that his heart had changed. And Paul proved himself to be a faithful Christian. But that's not all; he not only became a believer who spread the gospel far and wide to the Gentile world, he also became the person who wrote thirteen of the twenty-seven books in the New Testament. His new life in Christ affected the world for good, and his old life became something that was used powerfully to strengthen his testimony.

Tell me, what Christian with a sane mind would look down his or her nose at Paul today?

Paul was given a chance, and he proved his faith in God. Surely we can agree that Paul's past deeds were as bad as, or even worse than, those of the redeemed drug addicts, thieves, and even murderers who some people in the Church have trouble accepting into fellowship. Anyone who is saved from sin, anyone who has been redeemed, deserves a chance to be accepted by other believers. All believers should make it a practice to welcome redeemed ones with open arms and encourage them to grow and flourish in their new lives in Christ.

The God of the entire universe, our Creator, the only one who is holy and pure, and perfect in all of His ways, chose to love us all unconditionally. Now it is time for us to do the same for those He has saved. Now is the time to return the love God gives to us by loving others like Jesus loves them.

How is it that some believers think they can ever become holier than others based on the categorization of sins or whose present or past sins may be more numerous? To be a Christian means to be Christ-like. If we are imitating Christ, if we are indeed Christians, we will not allow ourselves to develop hypocritical attitudes. Instead, we will be able to both identify and avoid hypocrisy, and we will love one another like Jesus loves us.

Dear one, avoid the "H" word at all cost.

CHAPTER 16

DIFFICULT PEOPLE

THERE ARE TIMES in our lives when we will run into difficult—or just plain mean—people. There is no way to avoid them. And how we react to them can range from one end of a spectrum to the other.

At one end of the spectrum that I'm talking about is *placid submission* to difficult people and their opinions—where we simply cave in and do nothing to confront them or their views (let them walk all over us again and again). At the other end is *a stand of defiance and acts of retribution*—where we plant our feet in the ground and battle it out with them from the first contact (make sure they "get what they deserve").

When we experience the actions of difficult people, our first reaction may be to lash out at them. That is a common, basic, and human response that anyone who has battled against the flesh is personally familiar with. It's hard not to immediately attempt to defend or justify ourselves when dealing with difficult or mean people—especially when they verbally attack us.

But as Christians, we have choices. And the responses we choose should be positioned somewhere between the two extremes and always seasoned with forgiveness and grace. God will help us choose proper responses if we allow Him to do that; and depending on the actions we choose, our experiences with difficult people can yield surprising results.

One day a lady came into a beauty salon where I worked and asked me to cut her hair. Her name was Susan. I cut it exactly the way she instructed. She paid and left the salon appearing to be pleased with her haircut. Imagine my surprise when a few weeks later she came bursting through the door yelling at me and telling me that I had totally messed up her hair. (Her words were not that nice, but you get the idea.)

She began to call me every name in the book, swearing at me while her eyes darted in every direction. I was doing a client's hair at the time, and the upset woman started telling my client that she would never let me touch her hair again. Yet at the same time she was demanding that I cut it again for free to make it right. She claimed one side of her hair was much shorter than the other, although it certainly was not.

But the customer is always right, you know, so I cut it the way she said it needed to be cut. I was in tears the whole time I was cutting because she was still yelling profanities at me and calling me terrible names. By the time I finished, one side was definitely shorter than the other, but she insisted that it wasn't.

I had never been so embarrassed. And when she walked out of the beauty shop that day I determined to never give her another haircut as long as I lived.

I didn't see her again for a long time, but one day she came back to the shop. This time she was coming to use the tanning bed, and I had to turn it on for her. I could feel my blood pressure rising the moment she walked through the door. But as I watched her walk over to the desk to sign in, something strange happened in my heart. I was suddenly overwhelmed with compassion for her. I wondered what this lady had been through to cause her to be so hateful.

My mind then flashed back to a night prior to experiencing Susan's abusive behavior, when I and another lady, Leah, were working late. We finally finished cleaning before locking up and leaving the shop. When we walked outside we noticed another car in the parking lot. Leah turned to me and asked if we could have left anyone inside, and I told her I didn't think so. But I wasn't sure, so we went back inside and started checking all the tanning beds.

We came to a door that was still locked, and Leah started knocking on it loudly; but there was no answer. We had no way to open the door, so Leah grabbed a short ladder, climbed up, and looked over the top of the wall of the tanning booth.

She gasped and said, "It's Susan, and she's not moving, and she looks blue!"

Leah managed to reach the lock on the inside and unlock the door. When we opened the door we were both terrified. Susan lay there like a corpse. She didn't appear to be breathing, and she was very bluish in color. Leah grabbed her arm and began to shake her. Slowly, she raised her head and looked at us.

Leah said, "We are closing, you have to go home now."

Susan crawled out of the tanning bed, got dressed, and left without saying a word to us. Neither of us had any idea how long she had been in there. It had been a very busy day with customers coming and going, and we never even thought to check that tanning bed before leaving. It was a good thing we noticed her car.

Leah and I both knew at the time that Susan was under the influence of some kind of drug. And then, thinking back on that night, I started understanding that she also could have been under the influence of something the day she attacked me and demanded another haircut.

I had no idea what her reaction would be when I approached her to sign her in. But I cautiously walked to the desk with that past experience in mind. Then I remembered something I once heard Joyce Meyer say.

She said, "Hurting people hurt people."

After thinking about that, I looked Susan in the eye, and simply said, "Susan, do you know how much Jesus loves you?"

As I braced for the worst, she looked up at me, and tears began to roll down her cheeks. She said, "How could He love me? No one does."

I said, "That's not true at all. Jesus loves you, and I do, too."

She started to cry even more, so I asked her to come and sit down with me so we could talk.

I began to tell her how Jesus came to die for her sins on the Cross, and how He loved her with a love so powerful it couldn't be comprehended. She seemed to hang on every word as I continued to share the gospel message with her. Deep down I knew she had problems—and probably more issues going on in her life than I could even imagine. I was still hurt by the humiliation she had caused me, but Jesus had forgiven me for my many sins, so I was willing to forgive her as well.

I asked Susan if she would like to accept Jesus as her Savior, turn from her sin, and follow Him. She said, "Yes I would."

Tears of joy began to flow from her eyes as we prayed together. Then she grabbed me and hugged me so tightly that I could barely breathe. She thanked me over and over again for sharing Jesus with her, and she even apologized for the hateful and hurtful words she spoke to me before. It was an amazing experience.

"Hurting people hurt people."

It is so true. Many people who are hurting are not willing to let other people know about their problems, but because of all the hurt they are trying to bury and hide, they will often lash out at others. Sometimes they do that to keep other people from getting too close, because they don't want to be hurt again. At other times their action is a disguised, unconscious cry for help. Either way, though, people who are hurting tend to hurt others with their own actions.

In dealing with the actions of difficult people, we should try to look beyond the offense and seek to understand the reasons for their actions. That is often easier said than done, of course—especially in the heat of the moment. But what if we take the time to step back and look at that difficult person through the eyes of Jesus? That will surely help us.

What if we always allow the Lord to show us the root of the problem, and then in love allow Him to give us healing words to speak into that person's life and lead that difficult person to the ultimate heart-mender? There's no telling how many escalating situations we will diffuse, and how many lost souls we will lead to Christ, if we always do that. We may even make a great friend in the process!

I didn't see Susan for many months after praying for her in the beauty shop. But one day, when I least expected it, she came through the door with a huge smile on her face. I almost didn't recognize her. She was so nicely dressed! She had on makeup, and her hair was well groomed. Her whole countenance seemed to just glow. And as she smiled at me, she was almost running to get to where I was.

"Donna!," she exclaimed, "Do you have a few minutes to talk?"

I did, so we went back to those same chairs in the back of the shop where she gave her heart to Christ.

She said, "I just want to thank you for sharing Jesus with me. He has changed my whole life! I took your advice and started attending an Assemblies of God church. I was delivered from drugs and baptized in the Holy Spirit!"

"Oh Susan, that is great news." I responded. "I am so excited for you!"

She quickly said, "That's not all! God introduced me to a wonderful, godly man in that church, and we started dating. He loves the Lord with all his heart, and he treats me like a princess!"

She gave me another big, bright smile, winked at me, and said, "Donna, we just got married, and we're moving to Texas! I stopped by here today because I told him he had to meet the young lady who cared enough about me to attempt to rescue me from myself—the one who saw something in me that I never could have seen, the one who showed me love and acceptance even after I treated her terribly, and the one I probably hurt badly."

She continued and said, "Donna I want to sincerely thank you from the bottom of my heart for believing in me."

I could only cry. We hugged for quite some time, and she brought her new husband into the shop to meet me. He was a very charming man who seemed to be totally submitted to God, and very much in love with Susan! I was so incredibly happy for them. They were so excited to begin their life together with Jesus in the very center of their marriage.

As I watched them leave the shop, hand in hand, I began to think back to the day when Susan had called me every hateful name she could possibly dream up. Oh how I wanted to share a few choice words with her that day! I also thought about the night we found her passed out in the tanning bed, and how terrified Leah and I had been. Her drug abuse could have ended her life. Then I reflected on the day when she and I sat behind that desk and prayed for her salvation.

Things could have gone so much differently. It was so hard to hold my tongue in the heat of the moment, but because I remembered the phrase, "hurting people hurt people," I was able to find a little compassion in my heart and the courage to share Jesus with one so lost.

Clearly, everyone will not react the way Susan did when we share the gospel message. Witnessing to some people can most certainly yield the opposite effect. But *what if*—what if just one hurting person is snatched from the fire through the words of our witness?

Listen to the words of Jesus as quoted by His disciple, John:

"For God so loved the world that he gave his one and only Son, that whoever believes in him shall not perish but have eternal life. For God did not send his Son into the world to condemn the world, but to save the world through him." (John 3:16-17)

What if only one person responds to our preaching and is saved? Was it worth all our time spent ministering to others who were not moved? What if only one person in the world will respond from this day forward to our witness of the gospel message? Is it worth the time spent by all the millions of believers in the world continuing to witness God's Word? The answer should be evident.

What if only one were to respond to Christ's ministry? Would He have given His life for only one? And what if that one were you?

The answer is clear; so the value of even one soul rescued from destruction is inestimable. People (the crown of His earthly creation) are so valuable to God that He is interested in us rescuing each and every difficult person from his or her own destruction.

I can't tell you how much love and joy this one experience I just related to you brought to my life. Do you know a difficult person you could rescue today? Do your very best to do that. Lead that person to the solution—Jesus.

By the way, as Christians we are called upon to examine ourselves.[31] It would be good for you and me both to ask ourselves,

---

31 Lamentation 3:40; I Corinthians 11:28; 2 Corinthians 16:5.

"Am I a difficult person?" If we find the answer to that question is, yes, the solution for that condition is the same regardless of whether it applies to others or to us.

CHAPTER 17

AND IN CLOSING . . .

IN SUMMING UP everything I've attempted to say in this book I will leave you with two thoughts:

First, ministry and outreach is hard. It's time-consuming. It's frustrating. And the work sometimes brings heartache and pain to the one doing the ministering.[32]

I don't say these things to discourage you but to inform you and prepare you for what is to come if you faithfully follow Christ and do what He has called you to do. There is no higher calling than to represent Jesus and be His hands reaching out to people in need. But just as Jesus, His disciples, and all others who

---

32 "Then Jesus said to his disciples, 'If any of you wants to be my follower, you must turn from your selfish ways, take up your cross, and follow me. If you try to hang on to your life, you will lose it. But if you give up your life for my sake, you will save it. And what do you benefit if you gain the whole world but lose your own soul? Is anything worth more than your soul? For the Son of Man will come with his angels in the glory of his Father and will judge all people according to their deeds'" (Matthew 16:24-27 NLT).

have represented Him have known both disappointment and opposition, so will we.

And all who truly follow in the paths God prepares for ministry will know what it is to live a life of labor. Labor is work. And work is all the things that word infers. If you are not willing to work, you will not be successful in ministry.

Second, while the ministry into which God calls you may be challenging, it also will be rewarding beyond description. The ultimate reward prepared for Christ's followers is out of this world—literally.[33]

There is nothing better than praying with someone to accept Jesus as Savior. It brings us such joy to pray for people to be healed or delivered from bondage. And it is so fulfilling to be able to lead people into receiving the baptism of the Holy Spirit. But there's more. Our ultimate reward for being faithful in ministry will be given to us in Heaven, and it will be greater than anything we will ever experience here on earth!

As a representative of Christ, there may be times when you feel despised by the entire world, and there may be other times when you feel as if the whole world loves you. Never let either of those times go to your head or affect your resolve to minister to others faithfully as you humbly walk with and work for God.

People may hurt you and reject you—sometimes unintentionally but sometimes on purpose. Love them anyway.

---

33 "Rejoice in that day and leap for joy, because great is your reward in heaven" (Luke 6:23a).

There is a potential for hurt feelings or offenses to arise whenever people are involved in personal interactions. Always do your best to overcome those feelings. People are important to God. He loves people. Consider what a great honor it is, and what a great responsibility God has given you, to represent Him before them!

Remember that every ministry opportunity is absolutely special to God. He is no respecter of persons. While the Lord desires to minister to everyone in attendance in a large gathering, He is just as motivated to minister to just one person in a small gathering, or in a one-on-one meeting. I have spoken to congregations of ten or less, and I have spoken to congregations of over 1,000. After all those experiences I can honestly say that I would never value one opportunity over the other no matter how large or small the congregation. In fact, I especially love one-on-one ministry.

Several years ago, the Holy Spirit impressed upon my heart to pray for someone I didn't even know. She was a well-known women's minister, and I had heard of her but had never seen her in person. I sent her a prayer in a private message on Facebook, but I still had this feeling that I needed to pray for her in person. I didn't think that could possibly happen because we lived over 900 miles away from each other.

She wrote back to me and thanked me for the prayer, and we talked about how it would be great to meet in person someday. A few days later she sent another message and told me she would be speaking at a women's conference in Iowa, and it was very close to where I lived. It was uncommon for her to come to Iowa—she had only been there once before—so I planned to go to that conference; and I did get the opportunity to pray for her in person, praise God!

She spoke some words to me that day that I will never forget. I have held onto them tightly because they impacted me so powerfully. Because of what she was facing in her life at that particular time, she said she really needed me to be at that conference, and she knew God had sent me there for her.

She said, "Donna, God trusts you, and that is no small thing. He knew He could count on you to obey Him, to listen to His voice, and to follow His instructions."

"God trusts me?" I thought to myself. "Wow!" Those words gripped my heart as I began to think about the great responsibility I felt to continue to earn His trust.

I wonder how often we stop and think about the privilege God has given us to speak to others on His behalf. Tell me, when you get that gentle nudge in the supermarket to speak to strangers and ask them how they are doing, are you obedient?

When you meet people who are going through a struggle or trial, and God places you in their paths, are you obedient to share Jesus with them?

No matter how big or how small you feel your platform of ministry is, you can believe that God has put you there and presented you with that opportunity to minister because He knows He can trust you. Don't sell yourself, and especially God, short. Perhaps He has put you in the position at that precise moment to snatch a soul from the very flames of hell.

Every single soul is precious to God. Every time I lead a person to Christ, I always look to heaven and say "Thank you, Jesus, for TRUSTING me with this person's life and destiny!"

If we have truly learned to be obedient in following the leading of the Holy Spirit, God knows that He can trust us regardless of the type of ministry He has given to us—or regardless of the number of souls He has placed before us in ministry. We may not have what we consider to be a large platform for ministry, but if we are faithful and obedient He will trust us and prosper our work for Him. What an honor we have, and what an amazing thing to think that the God of the whole universe would trust us to minister to others, each of whom is so important to Him that, as I alluded to earlier, Jesus would go to the Cross even for that one soul.

As I bring this book to a close, I want to expand a little more on the topic of rejection. I want to assure you that you can triumph over it.

I know from my own experience, from what I've learned in my discussions with other believers, and from what I've read of the experiences of others, that as a person who feels the Lord calling you to minister to others, you will likely, at some time, experience a feeling of being rejected.

Perhaps your feeling of rejection will be caused by the actions or words of someone the Lord is calling to repentance through your ministry. Perhaps it will come from someone who is close to you—even a friend or family member. But when you feel rejected remember this: God loves you! God wants to use you! And He will receive you and honor your efforts when no one else will.

King David knew rejection, and he had times of great sorrow over it. But he expressed his faith in God. Among many other thoughts birthed out of a heart that was determined to follow God—thoughts that he recorded in the twenty-seventh Psalm—he wrote this:

> *Though my father and mother forsake me, the Lord will receive me.*
>
> (Psalm 27:10)

David was so determined to remain faithful to God that even rejection by his own father and mother would not dissuade him.

Know who you are in Christ! Have confidence and trust in what He has asked you to do. While you are serving Him, no matter the type of that service, remember to put your personal relationship with Him first. Stay rooted and grounded in the Word of God so you won't be deceived. Study it and become mature in Christ.

Also, make sure you have an intimate prayer life. And when temptations come—and trust me, they will—look for the ways of escape.[34] God has already provided them for you. Take them.

---

34 "No temptation has overtaken you except what is common to mankind. And God is faithful; he will not let you be tempted beyond what you can bear. But when you are tempted, he will also provide a way out so that you can endure it" (1 Corinthians 10:13).

Stand unwavering in your faith knowing that God is your firm foundation. Make the choice to love others, even when you think it's too hard to do.

And remember that the life you live before others is just as important as the words you share with them. The world is watching you to see if you are different and whether or not your life matches up with your message. Don't become one of those who have for one reason or another fallen to the wayside or laid down their ministries when hard times or temptation came. Be faithful!

The apostle Paul was a faithful follower of Christ. He knew the struggles associated with Christian ministry—even some that you and I may never experience ourselves. He wrote the following, instructive, and encouraging words from his prison cell. And now we receive and respond to them today.

As a prisoner for the Lord, then, I urge you to live a life worthy of the calling you have received. Be completely humble and gentle; be patient, bearing with one another in love. Make every effort to keep the unity of the Spirit through the bond of peace. There is one body and one Spirit, just as you were called to one hope when you were called; one Lord, one faith, one baptism; one God and Father of all, who is over all and through all and in all.

But to each one of us grace has been given as Christ apportioned it. This is why it says:

"When he ascended on high, he took many captives and gave gifts to his people."

(What does "he ascended" mean except that he also descended to the lower, earthly regions? He who descended is the very one who ascended higher than all the heavens, in order to fill the whole universe.) So Christ himself gave the apostles, the prophets, the evangelists, the pastors and teachers, to equip his people for works of service, so that the body of Christ may be built up until we all reach unity in the faith and in the knowledge of the Son of God and become mature, attaining to the whole measure of the fullness of Christ.

Then we will no longer be infants, tossed back and forth by the waves, and blown here and there by every wind of teaching and by the cunning and craftiness of people in their deceitful scheming. Instead, speaking the truth in love, we will grow to become in every respect the mature body of him who is the head, that is, Christ. From him the whole body, joined and held together by every supporting ligament, grows and builds itself up in love, as each part does its work. (Ephesians 4:1-16)

Christ descended to Earth to become God in the flesh—God living among men. He paid the awful sacrifice for our sins by dying on the Cross. He arose triumphantly from the grave and ascended back into Heaven. But that was not the end of His plan. He also established His followers as bearers of the Good News that we still carry to others today.

According to Paul, Jesus gave His followers to the world as gifts. He gave the world apostles, prophets, evangelists, pastors, and teachers for the express purpose of equipping His people for doing works of service that would result in the whole body of Christ being built up in unity, faith, and knowledge of Christ—the Way, the Truth, and the Life.[35]

Following Paul's line of reasoning, Christian leaders have a responsibility to prepare others for "works of service." The phrase *works of service* means nothing if it does not mean *ministering to the needs of others.* So Paul understood that God's expectations for Christian ministry include but extend well beyond the scope of work assigned to apostles, prophets, evangelists, pastors, and teachers. All believers are called to and should be equipped to represent Christ to those in need. And there is no greater need on earth than for people to come to know and grow in Christ.[36]

All followers of Christ are called to represent Him in the world. Works of service—callings to minister to the needs of others—should never simply be relegated to pastors, evangelists, and other people in the Church given specific titles and positions.

In the passage from *Ephesians* quoted, above, Paul refers to the importance of Christian growth and maturity. But in doing so he highlights the reason for that needed growth. He talks about the

---

35 "Jesus answered, 'I am the way and the truth and the life. No one comes to the Father except through me'" (John 14:6).

36 I quote the words of Assemblies of God Minister, Author, and Editor L. Edward Hazelbaker. Used by permission.

whole body of Christ (the Church), its relationship to God, its need for unity and strength, and its work.

Paul's words infer the importance of the work given to all Christians to represent Christ in the world. Like our earthly bodies, each part of the Body (the Church) must do its work in order for the overall body to function properly. Each Christian is pictured as being a part of the whole body of Christ in the world. That body is a living, breathing organism, and you, dear Christian, are a part of that body.

We have a tendency to rank ourselves and others in order of our feelings of importance in the Church. But truthfully, each and every part of a body exists for a reason; and Christ orders His Body with wisdom according to His will. Don't fall into thinking the more visible ministries are more important than others. They're not more important, they're just more visible.

As a Christian, you are a part of the Church, and if you fail to do the work God has called or is calling you to do, the overall work and mission of the Church will suffer.

The Body of Christ has a mission. That means it's time for each of its parts to do its work. All of us—all of the individual parts that make the Church function—need to get to work. I encourage you to listen to God and be faithful in ministry.

I love you and I'm praying for you as you pursue God's call on your life.

EPILOGUE

AS I SAID before, you could never make a better decision than to yield your life to God's plans. Along with those words I also encouraged you to allow God to work in you and through you. I counseled you to allow Him to do what He wants to do. Have you done that? Do you really know Jesus? Have you surrendered your life completely to Him and allowed the Lord to accomplish His will in your life?

If not, I plead with you to do it now. Once again I tell you that Jesus loves you, and He wants to forgive you and unite you with our heavenly Father. Wander no more in regret and confusion. Allow the Lord to restore you and reveal to you the wonderful plan He has for the rest of your life.

If you are ready to take the step of repenting of past sins and failures, and if you are ready to commit yourself to knowing and following the Lord as he directs you by His Holy Spirit, pray this prayer with me:

Dear Jesus, I know I have failed you, and I've made mistakes in my life. I believe you are the Son of God, and I believe you can wash away all my mistakes and failures. Please forgive me. As I turn now from my sin, help me to discover and follow the plans that you have for my life. I know you want the best for me. I accept you as my loving Savior and Friend. Lead me to the Father, and fill me with your Holy Spirit. In Your precious Name I pray, Jesus. Amen.

If you just prayed that prayer and meant those words with all your heart, I want to say, "Welcome to the Family of God!"

Congratulations! Now go live for God; further educate yourself in the gospel message; and take the good news to others.

JOY FOR ALL SEASONS
Carol McLeod

Imagine reading a book that is so much more than written words on a page but, instead, an invitation to experience exuberant joy! Simply imagine the sweet hope that comes from reading about the patience, the gladness and the excitement that is nestled within one woman's heart. Imagine! You have just imagined the devotional book entitled, "Joy for All Seasons" written by best-selling author, blogger, speaker, radio host, TV host and Bible teacher, Carol McLeod.Her capacity for joy and her resolve to trumpet the bidding to embrace joy in every week of the year is not for the faint of heart. This weekly summons into His presence is filled with rich experiences, with heart-felt celebration and with an intimate knowledge of what it takes to walk with God.

ISBN: 9781610361965

GIVE ME 40 DAYS
Freeda Bowers

If you take a moment to think about all that God has told each believer to do, it is almost overwhelming: Go into all the world and preach the gospel, feed the poor, clothe the naked, visit the prisoner and so much more. However, these "works" are to be an outpouring of our relationship with Christ, not a replacement of our devotion and time with Him.

That outpouring only comes through prayer.

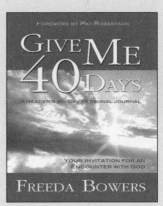

ISBN: 9781610360913